About the author

Sibel Hodge is the author of bestselling romantic comedy *Fourteen Days Later*. She has 8 cats and 1 husband. In her spare time, she's Wonder Woman! When she's not out saving the world from dastardly demons, she writes books for adults and children.

Her work has been shortlisted for the Harry Bowling Prize 2008, Highly Commended by the Yeovil Literary Prize 2009, Runner up in the Chapter One Promotions Novel Comp 2009, nominated Best Novel with Romantic Elements in 2010 by The Romance Reviews, and a Finalist in the eFestival of Words 2013. Her novella *Trafficked: The Diary of a Sex Slave* has been listed as one of the Top 40 Books About Human Rights by Accredited Online Colleges.
For more information, please visit
www.sibelhodge.com

D1399498

Also by Sibel Hodge

"And once the storm is over, you won't remember how you made it through, how you managed to survive. You won't even be sure, whether the storm is really over. But one thing is certain. When you come out of the storm, you won't be the same person who walked in. That's what this storm is all about."
— Haruki Murakami

Chapter 1

Do you believe that everything happens for a reason? Mum did, in a big way, although I never quite got it, and I'd thought about it a lot in the year since the accident. I mean, if good things happen, then yes, maybe you can find a reason. But when bad things happen to people, tragedies, how can there be a good reason for it? It was a question that stayed in my mind all the time these days, but I was still no closer to justifying a reason for what had happened.

I was thinking about it again as I slid the key in my front door lock, head down, eyes averted from any possible neighbours watching, which had become my usual stance now. I took a deep breath and opened the door, knowing that Dad was home and bracing myself for him to ask about my day.

Slinging my school bag down on the floor and kicking off my shoes, I breathed out a heavy sigh of relief. One more day left of school. One more exam and then I'd be free of them all.

Dad poked his head out of the kitchen door with an encouraging smile. 'Hi, how was your day?'

I shrugged. What was I supposed to say? That I'd had yet another day of the taunts and whispered bitchings and the blatant name-calling: *ugly, scarface, weirdo, freak.* Their words echoed permanently in my ears.

Dad stood there with a quiet expectation, hoping I'd tell him things were looking up. That I was feeling better about everything. That I had friends again.

'It was OK,' I mumbled.

'Only OK?' He walked over to give me a hug, enveloping me with his arms and pulling me in tight.

I could smell his familiar odour of the outdoors and animals from his job as a vet at Longleat Safari Park. It was comforting somehow, familiar. I fought back the tears stinging my eyes. I was sick of crying about it all.

He rested his chin against the top of my head. 'Did the exam go all right? All the hard revision you've been putting in, I'm sure you thrashed it.'

'Yeah, well, it's not like I've got a life, is it? What else is there to do except school work and TV?' I tried to wriggle away. Next, he'd be telling me to get out more with my friends and go and do what other normal teenagers were doing. Except my friends weren't my friends anymore, and I was far from normal now.

He gave me a squeeze and pulled back, arms resting on my shoulders as he looked into my eyes, searching for something I couldn't tell him. 'Only one more exam left, Jazz, and then you'll be leaving. Have you thought about what you want to do next?'

I looked away at a spot on the carpet where a thread had come loose. Of course I'd thought about it. I wanted to get my GCSEs out of the way and do my A-Levels. I wanted to do a law degree and work for the Crown Prosecution Service. I wanted to stand up in the middle of a packed courtroom and fight for justice. Except that wasn't going to happen now. I couldn't stand in front of one person and hold my head up high, and no one was going to employ someone who looked like me.

The anger came bubbling to the surface again as I remembered I wasn't the old Jazz anymore. I was just a freak.

'Stop hassling me all the time.' I rushed past him and stormed up the stairs to my bedroom, slamming the door.

I threw myself on the bed and stared up at the luminous plastic stars on my bedroom ceiling that lit up at night. Mum had put them up there a few years before when she'd decorated because they reminded her of the night sky in Kenya, where she and Dad lived before I was born.

Mum, I miss you.

I felt a suffocating pain in my chest and turned onto my side to stare at the photo of her on my bedside table. If she were here, she'd know what to do. She'd give me good advice and warm smiles. She'd make me creamy hot chocolate with marshmallows on top. She'd dish out hugs and jokes and let me know everything was going to be OK.

I heard the doorbell ring downstairs and the sound of Dad's voice.

'Hi, Jazz,' Aunt Katrina called up to me.

Great. She was the last person I wanted to see at the moment. If I stayed up here long enough maybe she'd be gone by the time I went down. She was my mum's identical twin, and every time I looked at her it was like seeing a ghost. Sometimes I'd get home from school and she'd be sitting with Dad in the kitchen, chatting over a cup of coffee, and the breath would just evaporate from my lungs in a painful blow. Every time, for just a fleeting moment, I'd think Mum was back. That the accident didn't happen. And then the reality would sink back in again and I'd realise it was just Katrina.

'Hi,' I yelled back down, grabbing my chemistry textbook and notes and wiping away the tears that had started falling with the back of my hand. I already knew the text off by heart, but I needed something to distract the thoughts from tumbling in again. It was either that or watch TV, and I wasn't in the mood for watching perfect-looking people on their stupid programmes.

Later, as the light faded from the room, I glanced at the clock and saw two hours had passed. I hadn't heard Katrina go and I was dying to go to the toilet. If she heard me, I knew she'd call up to try and make me come downstairs for a chat. I was surprised Dad hadn't tried already. If I was quiet, I could make it up the corridor to the bathroom and back to my room before they even heard me.

Gripping the door handle, I pushed it down slowly, waiting for the small click as it opened. I padded barefoot down the hall, carefully avoiding the squeaky patch of floorboards outside Dad's bedroom. Their low voices wafted upstairs…

'When are you going to tell Jazz?' Katrina said.

I stopped at the sound of my name. I know they say that eavesdroppers never hear anything pretty, but there was nothing pretty about me, so what did it matter?

'I wanted to wait until she's finished her last exam. I don't want her worrying about this, too. She's under a lot of pressure, and I don't know how she's going to react,' Dad said.

'I think it's a good idea,' Katrina said. 'I think it will be the best thing for both of you.'

He sighed, like he often did these days. 'I've thought about this for months and I'm sure it's the right decision.'

'It is. You both need time to heal.'

What? What's a good idea?

'I think it's the only thing to do under the circumstances, but I don't think Jazz will see it like that,' Dad said.

Every muscle tensed as I stood there, straining my ears.

'When will you be going?' Katrina asked.

'In three weeks. I'm renting the house out. I'll give it a year and see what happens.'

'Well, I can't wait to come and see you when you've got settled in. I've always wanted to go to Africa on safari. All the stories you and Leigh have told me over the years make it sound amazing.'

I gasped.

Africa? What the hell is he going on about? We're not going to Africa!

Maybe I'd misheard. I crept back down the hallway to the top of the stairs, sitting softly on the top step. This couldn't be right. There must be some mistake.

'Since the accident, Richard and Jenna have been in constant touch,' Dad said. 'They were so sad about what happened to Leigh. They loved her, too. And the game reserve has just lost a vet, so it kind of seems like an opportunity has come up just at the right time, really.' Dad's voice was enthusiastic but laced with worry. 'Do you really think it's the right thing? I just don't know what do with Jazz anymore. I can't get her to open up. It's like she's sinking into this depression, and I can't seem to reach her. I think we need a new start away from all the memories.'

'I know. And I'm sure this is what you both need,' Katrina said. 'You and Leigh loved Kenya; maybe it will be cathartic for you to go back now.'

The anger that I'd felt earlier erupted into a volcano of bursting energy. No way. No way was I going to Africa. I stormed down the stairs and barged into the kitchen.

'I'm not going to Africa!' I yelled at Dad.

Katrina exhaled a sharp breath. 'I'm sorry,' she said, as if it was all her fault, but I couldn't even look at her.

Dad sat at the kitchen table, his tall frame suddenly looking small and defeated. He stared into my flashing eyes and gave me that look. The look I'd seen a million times since the accident. I could never quite work out what it was. Pity? Concern? Shame? Blame?

'I didn't want you to find out about it like this.' He pinched the bridge of his nose with his thumb and forefinger, shaking his head.

'What are you talking about?' One hand flew to my hip. 'How can we go to Africa? How can we leave this house? This is Mum's house!'

His hand dropped to the table lifelessly. 'But your mum isn't here anymore, sweetheart.' He tried to reach out and take my hand, but I snatched it out of reach.

'I know that!' I screamed, tears springing into my eyes.

'I think we need to get away,' he said. 'A place where you can make a fresh start.' He stood up and paced the floor, avoiding my gaze as his words poured out. 'It's not healthy for you to stay locked in the house all the time. You never go out; you've got no interest in anything. All you do is stay cooped up in that bedroom and it's not healthy. You don't even climb anymore, and you used to love doing that. I'm worried that you're not getting over this.'

I pointed to the scars on my face. Even though I'd had a fringe cut into my long blonde hair to cover the scars on my forehead, it did nothing to hide the angry pink slashes on my cheeks and nose. 'Would you want to go out looking like this? I've got a permanent reminder etched into my face. How can I get over it?' I snapped. 'Mum's grave is here. How can you leave that? Have you forgotten about her already?'

'Of course he hasn't, darling,' Katrina piped up, her eyebrows furrowed in a sympathetic frown. 'And your scars will fade in time.'

I choked back the tears. I wanted it to be Mum sitting there with Dad, instead of her double.

'They'll never fade!' I glared at them. 'And, I'm not going. I'm sixteen. I can legally leave home now. You can go to Africa on your own.'

'And how are you going to look after yourself?' Dad asked. 'You haven't got a job. You won't be able to afford a place to live.'

'So.' I shrugged and jerked my head at my aunt. 'I can get a job on the Internet so I don't have to see anyone. And I can live with Katrina.' I gave her a challenging stare through the tears, trying to focus. Even though being with her would be a constant reminder of what I'd lost, I didn't want to leave the only place I still felt a connection to Mum.

She stood up and walked towards me. 'Oh, darling, I'm sorry, but that's not possible.' She held her arms out, inviting a hug. 'It's only for a year, just to get some breathing space. When you come back, maybe you'll feel more confident about studying law again.'

I stepped back and she dropped her arms to her sides with a soft slap.

'This is all about you!' I turned towards Dad. 'You're just thinking about yourself. Anything so you can be with your stupid animals all day long. What about me? What about what I want?'

'Believe me, Jazz, this is all about you,' he said.

'How can you say that?' I spat. 'I don't even want to go there.' I dropped the hand from my hip and bunched it into a fist, nails digging into my palm.

Dad got to his feet, towering above me, giving me that look again. 'I've been offered a veterinary job at Richard and Jenna's game reserve. You know how much your Mum and I loved it out there, and I'm sure you will, too. It's an amazing opportunity. They've also been kind enough to give you a job there as a chambermaid. Hopefully, keeping busy with something will take your mind off things.'

My eyes widened. 'What?' But I didn't wait for him to answer. 'Don't you get it, Dad? I don't want people staring and laughing.'

'They won't laugh at you,' Katrina said.

'Yeah?' I sneered. 'Like the kids at school don't laugh at me, you mean?' No one looked at me and saw Jazz anymore. They just saw an ugly girl to make fun of. I glared at Dad. 'You know I don't want people to see me. How could you do this?' My voice cracked.

'You can't live the rest of your life locked up in a box,' he said. 'This is for your own good.'

I threw my hands up in the air. 'No, it's not, don't you see?'

Dad looked up at the ceiling, taking a deep breath. He stayed like that for a few minutes while I simmered away, trying to think of something to say to make him change his mind. When he finally turned back to me with a steady and determined gaze he said, 'I'm not saying that this is going to be easy, but you can't live in the past forever. I can't either. You need to let go and start to live again. We have to find something better, something happier in our future.' He paused to make sure I was listening. 'We're going to Africa and that's the end of it.'

He just didn't get it, though. It was all very well running away, but I couldn't run away from the thing I most wanted to. It's not like you can ever get away from yourself, is it?

Chapter 2

Over the coming weeks, I tried everything I could to change Dad's mind. I yelled and cried and gave him the silent treatment but nothing worked. He arranged for the house to be rented out, and I had to endure strangers poking their noses around while they scrutinised our house as a prospective place to live. Usually, I'd hide myself away on a bench in the far corner of the garden, head down, shivering in the wind until they'd gone. I think I hated him at that point. I couldn't understand how he could just leave everything behind. How he could leave the memories of us with Mum in this house and go to some stupid game reserve in the middle of nowhere. Why did he think that would help me move on?

Slowly and painfully our personal possessions were packed away to go into storage, but the worst thing was finally getting rid of Mum's belongings. All her lovely clothes that had remained in their wardrobe since the accident; her beloved vinyl record collection, her books, her makeup. It was like the final piece of her was being thrown away − a betrayal of her life, and it cracked my heart into a thousand pieces all over again.

It was my fault. That was the worst part.

If only I hadn't been running late for school she wouldn't have been driving too fast. If only I hadn't been rummaging around in my bag searching for my English homework, she wouldn't have been looking at me and telling me to put my seatbelt on. If only she hadn't been distracted by me, she would've noticed the red light and not driven through it. If only the lorry hadn't ploughed into our car and crushed her.

If only. If only.

The scars on my face were a constant reminder that I caused her death. I relived the scene again and again. The explosive sound as the other driver crashed into Mum's door. The windscreen crunching as we were pushed into a nearby tree, and then nothing but blackness. That was why I'd banned any mirrors from the house. I couldn't bear to look at myself, not just because of what I saw on the outside. I hated the inside more.

Jazz, the girl who caused her mum's death.

You know how it is when you listen to a recording of your voice and you think it doesn't sound anything like you? That's how it was when I looked in the mirror. I was trapped inside the face of a girl who wasn't me.

It wasn't supposed to be like this. It wasn't supposed to happen. No matter how many times Dad and Katrina told me it was an accident, that it wasn't my fault, I didn't believe them. I knew, and I knew they knew, too.

When it was time to go to the airport we left the house with two suitcases each. Dad lugged them out to Katrina's car and stared back at our home with a wistful expression as I wandered from room to room, saying goodbye to the memories we'd shared here as they filtered randomly into my mind, vivid scenes playing out as if they'd only happened yesterday…

The time when I was five years old and Mum patched up my knee after falling over the handlebars of my bike. The first day of secondary school, when I didn't want to leave her and she told me she'd bake my favourite cookies after school as a bribe. When I was thirteen and James Godfrey ignored me after our first kiss and I thought it was the end of the world, Mum was there dishing out the hugs and back-patting and advice about boys. How she'd always tried to get me to appreciate her beloved jazz music, when all I wanted to listen to was pop. All the rescue animals she brought home from the vet's surgery where she worked as a nurse. The waifs and strays she loved that I was always jealous of because she spent so much time with them.

'Jazz,' Dad called from outside. 'Come on, sweetheart, it's time to go. We don't want to miss the flight.'

You don't want to miss it, more like.

I touched my fingertips to my lips in a kiss and pressed them to the walls.

I love you, Mum. I'm not leaving you.

A tear snaked its way down my cheek and dropped onto the carpet.

Shuffling down the front steps, I climbed into the backseat of Katrina's car and shut the door. I turned my head to gaze out of the window at the house so I could avoid Katrina's concerned looks in the rearview mirror. As we drove away, I heard her and Dad chatting about the game reserve and how it had the 'Big Five', whatever that was. They droned on about the weather in Kenya and all sorts of other stuff that I didn't care about. I pulled my iPod out of my backpack and shoved the earphones in so hard it hurt, drowning them both out.

Katrina pulled up at the passenger drop off point at Heathrow Airport, and I watched the hordes of people rushing around with luggage, saying goodbye to friends and relatives, hurrying off to catch their flights. I envied them. I bet they felt safe and secure in their normal lives. I bet they had no idea how things could change in an instant.

Suddenly, I didn't want to leave Katrina. Even though I hadn't shown her much affection since Mum died, she was the closest thing I had to her now. I wrapped my arms round her waist and buried my head in her shoulder.

'It will be OK, you'll see.' She stroked my hair.

I sniffed hard, trying to stop my nose from running.

'Jazz, you're only sixteen. Your life is an open book, and you can write the pages any way you want,' she whispered as Dad grabbed the luggage. 'It's up to you how the story goes.' She held me tightly. 'You know, sometimes it's the things you can't change that end up changing you.' She squeezed me tighter.

'We'd better check in,' Dad said after he put the suitcases

on a trolley.

She released me and gave him a quick hug. 'Go on, then. Off with you both. Have a lovely adventure.' She blinked quickly, trying not to cry.

We walked into the airport and I glanced back at her over my shoulder as she got into the car. Our eyes met, and she gave me a knowing look, like she knew the answer to some big secret I was yet to discover.

When we boarded the plane a few hours later, Dad gave me the seat next to the window. Maybe he thought I wanted to see the view as we landed in Africa, but that was the last thing on my mind. I sat down and closed the blind, not wanting to see my reflection staring back at me in all its ugliness through the glass. I stuffed my earphones in, turning my head to the blind to avoid Dad's hurt expression and the nosy, horrified stares of the other passengers.

We arrived in Nairobi in the late afternoon, and the first thing that hit me was the heat. Waves of suffocating hot air swept over me. By the time we'd walked to passport control the sweat was oozing from every pore. I stood in line behind Dad, staring at the ground, sighing and huffing every few minutes.

'Next,' a Kenyan customs officer called out in a loud voice.

I felt Dad tugging my arm, steering me towards the booth with him.

The man flicked through my passport as I stared at my trainers.

'Look at me, please,' he said.

I glanced up, focusing on a spot above the queue next to ours so I wouldn't have to look directly at him. I knew what he was thinking. The passport picture didn't look anything like me anymore. That was the old Jazz. The Jazz who people said was beautiful. The Jazz who obsessed about hair and designer fashion and the trendiest makeup to share with her friends.

I shuffled uncomfortably from foot to foot, feeling his

scrutinising gaze drilling into me. I heard an elderly woman in the queue next to me say to her travelling companion, 'And I bet she used to be so pretty, too.'

I could feel my temperature bubbling up to boiling point. She hadn't even tried to whisper it!

The customs man shook his head with a pitiful stare and stamped the passport, handing it back before he picked up Dad's.

After we got our luggage, I followed Dad into the arrivals hall where we were supposed to be met by Richard, Mum and Dad's friend and the owner of the reserve. I stayed behind Dad, cautiously taking in the smells and sounds and bustling of people carrying all sorts of oddly shaped luggage.

Dad spotted Richard and waved at him from across the crowd. He was in his late fifties with curly grey hair and a grey beard. He wore khaki shorts, his pockets bulging, and a khaki shirt. He had a deep tan and wrinkles at the corners of his sparkling blue eyes.

He grabbed Dad in a bear hug. 'Nathan. It's been too long. Far too long, my friend,' he said with a kind smile.

Dad nodded and patted his back. 'Well, you're a sight for sore eyes. You haven't changed a bit.'

Richard rubbed his stomach. 'Was I grey and fat sixteen years ago?' He laughed and turned to me, but I'd already lowered my eyes to his dusty, worn boots. 'And you must be Jazz. The last time you were here, you were still in your mum's belly.'

I nodded so I didn't have to say anything.

He bent his knees, lowering himself to my eye line so he could catch my gaze.

I looked away before I could see the signs of disgust.

'She's a bit shy,' Dad whispered, as if I wasn't standing there hearing him crystal clear.

I could've punched him. Shy didn't even begin to cover it.

Seeing I wasn't going to look at him, Richard stood upright again. 'Well, it's nice to meet you finally. I always hoped Nathan and Leigh would bring you out to see us before this.' He held his hand out.

I averted my eyes, reached out and shook it. 'You, too,' I mumbled.

'I'm so sorry about your mum. We loved her a lot,' Richard went on.

I didn't reply as thoughts of Mum filtered into my head again.

'Well, let's get going.' Richard took my two suitcases and pulled them along behind him with determined strides. 'We've got to get on a short flight before we get to the reserve. The pilot's ready and waiting for us.'

After heading back out onto the airstrip, we arrived at a small, battered private plane that looked like it was about a hundred years old. I wondered if it was safe enough to get us all the way there. It certainly didn't look like it, but then what did it matter if the thing crashed? Maybe it would be a good way out of my life. Sometimes I felt like I'd fallen overboard into a dark swampy river and a tide of hopelessness was dragging me under. Maybe I should just let it.

As we flew away from Nairobi and out into the country through pockets of bumpy turbulence, I stared out the window at the increasing bushland. Flat plains of dry earth, interspersed with trees, bushes, and village settlements with huts made of mud and grass. Nearing the game reserve, Dad pointed out herds of elephants, zebra, giraffes, and antelope down below with the excitement of a teenager. I wiped the sweat from my forehead with the palm of my hand and watched them all scatter away as the plane zoomed over their heads.

'Nearly there,' Richard, who sat next to the pilot, shouted over his shoulder at us.

Dad put his arm round my shoulder. 'How're you doing, sweetheart?' he whispered in my ear.

'I'm hot,' I mumbled.

'This is going to be great.' I could hear the smile in his voice.

'Hmmm,' I said, thinking the exact opposite.

'A new start, Jazz.' He pulled me towards him, kissing the top of my head.

'There's the airstrip.' Richard pointed to a long, dusty track in front of us in the middle of a wooded area.

'Surely we can't land there,' I whispered to Dad. 'There's no tarmac.'

Dad shrugged. 'This is Africa. They have to make do with what's available.'

I gripped the arm of my seat.

OK, maybe I was just joking about wanting the plane to crash.

After a bouncy landing, Richard, Dad, and I made our way to a dirty green Land Rover parked up alongside the airstrip.

God, how much longer till we get there?

I was hot, sweaty, tired and thirsty, and the journey seemed like it had been going on forever.

'Only another twenty minutes, then we'll get you settled. A nice cold drink and a shower will sort you out,' Richard said cheerfully as I clambered in behind Dad, carefully positioning myself so Richard couldn't look at me in the rearview mirror.

We bumped along a dusty track until we came to a tarmac road and we drove through a town.

'This is Jito,' Richard said to me. 'It means river in Swahili. We're lucky on our reserve because the river snakes through our land. Lots of watering holes for our game, and even in the driest times it's never completely dried up. Our turning is just a little further, but if you carry on this road there's a tribal settlement, then you'll come to our neighbouring reserve of Mumbi, and then onto the Masai Mara National Park.'

Ten minutes later, we drove off the tarmac onto a large dirt track for a few minutes and came to a metal gate and a wooden sign that announced our arrival at Kilingi Game Reserve. The reserve was fenced off with five metre high electric fences.

Richard unlocked the gates and we drove through.

'Look, Jazz.' Dad pointed out of the window. 'There's a warthog with some of its young.'

I stared in the direction he was pointing and saw a large animal with tough, blackened skin and long tusks hurrying away from us, her babies squeaking and scampering to keep up. I didn't share Mum and Dad's enthusiasm when it came to game animals. I mean, fluffy kittens and puppies and rabbits were OK, I supposed, but what was so special about a warthog?

'Those are the resort buildings.' Richard pointed off in the distance at some wooden buildings with wicker-type roofs. 'That's the reception, lounge, dining room, and bar. The swimming pool and spa are behind that.' He pointed to the right at some smaller individual buildings with balconies. Some were freestanding with others built into large trees. 'Those are the guest accommodation, but I'll take you on a grand tour later when you've freshened up a bit. Let's head for your quarters.' He turned to look over his shoulder at me and I stared at the floor. 'Just a word of warning for you, Jazz. There are a lot of dangerous animals out here, not to mention snakes and insects that could be deadly. Don't wander into the bush on your own, OK?'

As if I'd even want to wander around in this crap hole.

I nodded.

Richard took a left turn off the track and headed away from the buildings for another five minutes until we came to a small, basic-looking one-storey wooden building, built in the same style as the others he'd pointed out. It had large windows and a veranda with an outside seating area that overlooked the vast Kenyan plains.

The Land Rover rumbled to a stop and he and Dad leaped out. I picked at my thumbnail as I sat there staring at what was going to be my new home.

Dad had signed a year's contract, so we had to stay here for at least that long. We were in the middle of nowhere in oppressive heat. I seriously doubted that the house was going to have any mod cons, like air conditioning. It looked pretty unlikely there would be any internet connection here, either. Was there even a TV? And on top of that, there was no way I could avoid people if I was going to have to bump into guests every day when I cleaned their rooms. Dad had made it clear I was going to have to help pay my way.

I took a deep breath and stepped down from the Land Rover, wishing the year was already over. But if I knew then what I know now, I wouldn't have been so quick to wish my life away.

Chapter 3

'Your new home.' Richard nodded towards the house with a smile and strode up the few steps onto the veranda, carrying my two suitcases with ease.

Great.

I kept my head low and followed him and Dad.

Richard swung the flyscreen door open and it emitted a loud creaking sound. Setting the suitcases down, we stopped behind him.

I glanced around the long hallway with wooden floors which had several doors leading off either side, until my gaze rested on the thing that I'd been avoiding for so long.

A mirror.

I caught sight of my face. The pink and puckered scars that crisscrossed my pale skin. They were everywhere.

I gasped and jerked my eyes away, tears welling up once again. You'd think after all this time I'd be all cried out, but they never ceased to rear their ugly heads and threaten me with an overwhelming sense of loss.

Dad dropped his suitcases and I felt his hand gently rubbing my back. Even though I kept my gaze locked on the floor I could feel Richard's enquiring eyes questioning Dad's.

'Since the accident, we don't have any mirrors in the house,' Dad explained to Richard.

'I see,' Richard said thoughtfully. 'Well, I can do something about that.' He took the mirror off the wall, strode out to the Land Rover and came back mirror-less. 'Let me show you the rooms and I'll leave you to get settled. Bedrooms are up here.' He strode up the end of the hallway towards two doorways as I shrank into the wall, pressing my hot forehead against the coolness of it.

I glanced into the living room. There was a large navy blue sofa in the centre, facing French doors onto the veranda. A ceiling fan whirred away above us. A wooden coffee table and wooden sideboard with a lamp on top were the only furniture. There was no TV. How was I going to fill my days and nights?

I walked to the French doors and stared out. Dry patches of bush mixed with longer green grasses covered the plains. In the distance, I could see the river Richard mentioned, and the silhouettes of drinking giraffes. There were pockets of thick trees and vegetation all around. The sky was bright blue and so perfectly cloudless it looked like it had been painted for one of those posters advertising exotic holidays. I saw a herd of elephants with a couple of calves in their midst. I stared at them until they became blurry shapes and I heard Richard call out a goodbye.

Dad appeared behind me, staring at the grey specks. 'Wow, our first day here and you've seen elephants already!' He rested his hands on my shoulders. 'People pay thousands to stay here and see them. I'd say that made you a pretty lucky girl.'

My muscles tensed.

Lucky? What planet is he living on?

'Come and check out your room.' He grabbed my hand and led me to what would be my bedroom.

It was sparsely furnished like the lounge. A wooden double bed with mosquito netting draped around it that hung down from the ceiling. White cotton sheets. A small wooden bedside table and a wooden wardrobe. A ceiling fan. No TV.

'There's no TV here,' I said, walking towards the window that led out to more endless boring bush.

Dad chuckled. I hadn't heard that sound in a long time. 'Who needs a TV when you've got all this to look at?' He swept a hand towards the window. 'Let's get unpacked and then Richard's going to meet us at the lodge and give us a tour. Looks like it's changed a lot since I was last here.

There's a water cooler in the kitchen if you want a drink.'

'I don't want to go to the lodge.'

'You've got to do it some time and it might as well be now. I'm not having you hiding out in this house for the next year. And besides, you'll be working up there so it will be nice to get to know everyone, won't it?' He paused. 'Look, these people aren't going to judge you, they're our friends.'

'They're your friends, not mine.'

He sighed. 'This is a fresh start for us. Let's begin to enjoy it.' And with that his footsteps disappeared into his own bedroom next door and I heard him opening the cupboard doors and unpacking.

I took the photo of Mum that always had pride of place next to my bed from my backpack and kissed it, putting it down on the bedside table. Moving the mosquito netting out of the way, I flopped onto the bed with my head resting in my hands, staring at a black spot on the floorboards that looked like a squashed bug. Even though I was thirsty, I couldn't bring myself to go into the kitchen. I wanted to stay here in the sanctuary of my room. Forever. Maybe I'd die of dehydration. Who cared anyway? Dad certainly didn't. All *he* cared about was those stupid animals of his. But then, who could blame him? If I was him I wouldn't care about me, either.

We got into the dusty green Land Rover that Richard had left for us to use and headed towards the lodge. In the middle of this primitive bush, it was strange to see what looked like a luxury resort, perfectly blending into the countryside with its quaint wooden huts.

Parking next to another couple of Land Rovers with *Kilingi Game Reserve* written on the side, we walked into the A-frame reception building that had a thatched roof. Two ceiling fans whirring above us created a welcome breeze.

A short woman with long grey hair in a plait tapped away on a laptop on the reception desk. She had a pen tucked behind her ear and a frown of concentration on her face. And the weirdest thing was she had a baby baboon wrapped around her. The baboon's arms and legs were clinging on to her, and it was watching everything she did with huge, inquisitive eyes. The woman looked up when she heard us approach and broke into a big smile.

'Nathan, you're here!' She smiled and made her way around the desk.

I peeked from behind my long fringe, stealing a quick glance as she hugged Dad.

'Good to see you, Jenna.' Dad attempted to hug her back but the baboon was in the way. He laughed and stroked the baboon's head. 'This must be Bobo, who you've told me so much about.'

She smiled and stroked Bobo on the back as the baboon stared inquisitively at me. 'The one and only.' She turned her attention to me.

I dropped my gaze to the floor.

'I'm Richard's wife, Jenna. You must be Jazz,' she said.

Before I knew what was happening she crushed me in a big hug, complete with baboon.

'Lovely to meet you.' She released me just as quickly and nodded down to the baboon. 'Bobo was found abandoned by some farmers a few months ago, so we've been looking after her until she gets old enough to be released onto the reserve.'

I stole a glance at Dad as my eyes widened. This was crazy. Jenna had a pet baboon? What about germs?

Bobo reached out her hand and touched my face, staring with huge eyes that looked spookily human.

I shrank away from her.

'Oh, that's just her way of saying hi,' Jenna gushed. 'She likes you!' She took Bobo's hand and put it back round her neck. 'Let's go and find Richard and we can show you around. It's changed quite a lot since you were here, Nathan. And I'm sure Jazz would love to see her new home.'

Yeah, I'd just love it. Not.

She headed out through some double doors at the back of the building and we found ourselves in an oasis of lush garden overlooking a kidney-shaped swimming pool that had been made to look like a lagoon with rocks dotted around it and a waterfall at one end. Empty sunbeds with thick cushions were arranged on the terrace.

'All the guests are out on game drives or walking safaris at the moment, so it's pretty quiet.' Jenna led us past an open wooden building with a large roof. 'This is the outside bar area. There's an inside bar for the winter months when it can get a bit chilly out here. Ah, there you are, Richard.'

Richard stood behind the bar, chatting with a tall black man in a black and blue uniform. I hung back by the doorway, not wanting to attract any attention to myself.

'All settled in?' Richard asked Dad.

'Getting there.' Dad grinned. 'It's strange, it feels like I've never been away.'

Jenna made her way over to me with a look of concern on her face as she stroked Bobo. 'Are you OK, Jazz?'

I mumbled a reply and nodded.

'I bet you want to see your veterinary office, don't you?' Richard asked Dad.

His eyes lit up. 'Lead the way!'

I followed them to yet another wooden building behind the lodge. Richard pulled a key out of his pocket and unlocked the door, handing the key to Dad. Inside there was a large stainless steel table in the middle of the room with a moveable light above it, glass-fronted cupboards full of drugs, reference books on a shelf, and a desk to one corner.

Dad peered around with a smile of approval.

'Do you know much about game reserves?' Jenna asked me.

I shook my head.

'We're a Big Five reserve,' she said proudly. 'Which means you can find lion, leopard, rhino, buffalo, and elephant here. Your Dad will be responsible for treating any injured animals on the reserve, and sometimes the local livestock. He'll be collecting blood samples to monitor any spread of diseases, doing vaccinations, and helping us with relocated animals. We're interested in setting up breeding programmes for rare species, too, so he'll be heading up that side of things.' She reached out and touched Dad's arms. 'Oh, it's so good to have you back.'

'I think there will be plenty to keep you busy.' Richard clapped Dad on the back. 'We've got a lot more animals than we had when you were last here.'

'The reserve is pretty self-sufficient,' Jenna went on to me. 'We've got a huge veggie garden and livestock area. Even Internet, when the damn thing is working.' She chuckled and shrugged. 'Well, this is Africa.'

At least that's something.

'You'll be able to email Aunt Katrina and tell her how you're getting on out here. She'd like that.' Dad smiled at me.

I didn't return the smile. Why would I want to email her about this place? I didn't even want to be here.

'Why don't we leave the men here and I'll show you one of the guest rooms so you can see where you'll be working.' Jenna patted my arm and disappeared out the door as Bobo looked at me over her shoulder.

I gave Dad a pleading look. *Please, I'm not ready for all this.*

He shook his head softly.

I sighed inwardly and followed in Jenna's footsteps.

As we walked along a stone path back towards the guest rooms on the other side of the lodge a huge party of people came walking towards us.

I bent my head and stared at the sand-coloured stone path.

'Afternoon!' Jenna called out to them. 'How was the safari? What did you see?'

I heard people saying how amazing it was. How they saw cheetahs and rhinos and one of them even caught sight of a leopard.

Whoopy do!

Standing behind Jenna, I stared at their feet. I could feel a familiar flush creeping up my neck to my face as I felt their eyes on me. I could tell what they'd be thinking. Ugly, scarface, freak.

Jenna seemed to chatter on to them for ages while I shuffled from foot to foot, until they finally made their way back to their rooms for a shower or to settle around the pool.

'Let's look at one of the treetop suites. They're my favourite.' Jenna headed towards a large wooden structure that was built into one of the trees. It had the same style of wicker thatched roof, a balcony with rustic wooden furniture, and large windows.

Unlocking the door, we entered a lounge with sumptuous cream sofas that looked as soft as marshmallows. There was a mixture of wooden and wicker furniture, along with various African tribal-looking pieces around the room. The balcony had a bird's-eye view over the vast savannah.

'We've had all sorts of film stars and famous people stay here over the years,' she said with a hint of pride as I followed her into the bedroom. 'Well, what do you think?'

'It's lovely,' I muttered. And it was. There was a sunken bath that you could sit in and gaze through the windows, and a shower and toilet with expensive-looking chrome fittings. It was luxurious, and a complete surprise to have such comfort and decadence out here. In another lifetime, maybe I'd have liked to come here on holiday.

'We'll go and eat dinner in the kitchen in a minute. I bet you're starving, aren't you? All the staff try and eat before the guests have their evening meal. Tomorrow you and your dad can go for a safari with Richard to familiarise yourself with some of the area. We've got sixty-four square miles of land, so it will take a lot of getting used to,' she babbled on. 'Then the next day you can start work here. You'll be changing the sheets and towels, cleaning the rooms, and making sure the guests have everything they need. How does that sound?'

It sounded like my worst nightmare.

'Fathiya, our head chambermaid, will show you the ropes for a while so you won't be thrown in at the deep end.'

I felt the weight of Jenna's gaze on me as I stared at the huge, perfectly made up bed, wondering how I was going to put the sheets on with such military precision. I could tell she expected me to reply, but I was pretty sure she wouldn't like to hear what I wanted to say.

Silence filled the room until she broke it with a chirpy, 'Let's get the others and see what's for dinner.'

The large kitchen was hidden from the guest areas, and as we all walked in a mixture of cooking aromas greeted us. My stomach rumbled. I hadn't eaten since nibbling on half a slice of toast before we'd left home that morning. Food didn't interest me these days.

A short black man with a huge grin on his face stood in the kitchen, lifting the lids of some boiling pans and checking the contents.

'This is Chef.' Jenna nodded towards him. 'His real name's Abena, but he likes to be called Chef.'

Chef turned round, all smile and teeth. 'Nice to meet you.'

I stared at my feet, not knowing where to look.

'It smells delicious, Chef,' Dad said.

Luckily, I was relieved from being scrutinised by Chef when the sound of a pot boiling over made him turn back to the industrial-sized cooker in a flash.

At one end of the room there was a long table with benches either side. Several men were already seated, dressed in khaki shirts and shorts identical to Richard's, eating and chatting.

My hands shook slightly and I felt my stomach lurch. Even though my shoulders were stooped and I stared at a large platter of what looked like some kind of barbequed birds on the stainless steel kitchen worktops, I knew they'd all be looking at me.

'Take a seat, you two,' Richard said to us. 'Let me introduce you to everyone.'

I stared at the salt and pepper mill on the table while Richard rattled off names that I would never remember, and saying whether the men were game rangers, trackers, or part of their anti-poaching patrols.

Jenna peeled Bobo's hands and feet off her and settled her on a chair. Bobo leaned over to me with her arms out, expecting to be picked up.

I shrank back and sat next to Dad on the very end of the table. He reached for my hand and gave it a quick squeeze.

Jenna carried the platter to the table. 'This is guinea fowl,' she said to me, then turned to the others. 'Come on, tuck in while it's hot!'

Dad reached past me and held hands with Bobo. 'Hello, little one.'

Bobo's eyes lit up and she clutched Dad's fingers, examining each one slowly before looking up at him with a quizzical expression.

Jenna sat down opposite me and offered me the platter as Bobo climbed round her neck again and rested her head on Jenna's shoulder. 'It's just like having a baby all over again.' She smiled affectionately at Bobo. 'Zach always wanted to hang onto my neck everywhere I went, too.'

Tentatively, I put some of the meat on my plate and turned my attention to picking at it, hunching over and letting my hair fall over my face.

'Zach must be, what, eighteen now?' Dad said to Jenna.

She nodded proudly. 'He's just like his father.' She winked at Richard.

'What, grey and fat?' Richard chuckled.

She tutted. 'No, always getting into mischief with the animals. He'll be here soon, he's just out leading a walking safari.'

Halfway through the meal, Jenna jumped up from the table to greet a guy who'd just come in. I stole a look at him out of the corner of my eye. He wore the same khaki uniform as the others. With short dark hair that was almost black, a deep tan that comes from working out in the sun every day, and broad shoulders, he was the type of guy that my friends and I would've swooned over if we'd seen him in a magazine. Back when I'd had friends, of course.

'Zach!' Jenna hugged him.

'Hey, Mum.' He grinned at her.

'Come and meet Jazz and Nathan.' She grabbed his hand and dragged him towards the table.

I shrank down further on the seat and tried to swallow a morsel of guinea fowl, but it was like my throat had suddenly constricted and it got stuck. I reached for my glass of water, not daring to look up at it for fear I'd see him staring at my scars with horror, but I misjudged where the glass was and knocked it over, spilling the contents on the platter and the table.

As the water ran towards me, I instinctively leaped up from my seat and swore inwardly. Not only had I ruined their dinner, but I'd now drawn unwanted attention in my direction.

I let out a cry of embarrassment and rushed towards the door, but as I passed Zach my gaze unwittingly caught his piercing topaz-coloured eyes, and I saw exactly what I was expecting in them: shock, disbelief, and pure disgust.

Chapter 4

The hot air hit me as I stumbled outside, tears blurring my vision. I didn't know where I was going; I just wanted to get away from all of them. I felt a pull on my arm and turned to see Dad, clutching me. 'Don't you remember what Richard said? Don't go off on your own. It could be dangerous.'

'Who cares?' I yelled at him. 'I'd be better off dead, anyway. Then you can go and look after your precious animals and it'll save you the embarrassment of having a freak as a daughter!' As the words tumbled out of my mouth I knew it was unfair, but I couldn't help it. No one could really understand. He'd done everything he could think of to try and make me feel better about myself, but I knew he'd never change how I felt. And on top of that, I knew he was still grieving for Mum, too. Sometimes I'd catch him staring at their wedding picture with so much regret and sadness it made my insides twist with pain.

He rested his hands on my shoulders and took hold of my chin, tilting it up to meet his face. Even though Dad and Katrina were the only people I could hold eye contact with these days, I still didn't like what I saw reflected in his eyes.

'You can't change the past, Jazz.'

I blinked and looked away, not wanting to hear it again. How I needed to move on. How I needed to get over everything and live again. Blah, blah, blah. It was just rubbish.

He exhaled a deep breath. 'Come on. It's been a long day. Why don't we head for bed? Everything will look brighter in the morning.'

I followed him to the Land Rover, wondering if he really believed that.

After the short drive back I had a shower, turning the tap to the coldest setting, but the water was still warm. I slid under the sheets, flicked off the light and listened to the sounds of the African plains. It seemed to be even noisier out here at night than during the day. Crickets, frogs, cicadas, the barking of some kind of animal, the roar of what I thought were lions, and the hysterical shrieking of hyenas. It was a million miles away from the odd bird song and traffic noise in Wiltshire.

I tossed and turned, trying to drown out the noise and find a cool spot on the bed. Even the ceiling fan didn't seem to be helping much. It was early in the morning before I fell into a restless sleep, but even then I was tormented with a recurring dream I'd had ever since the car crash. Mum and I were travelling in a car down a long country lane, except Mum wasn't driving, I was. As we rounded a blind corner, Mum was suddenly not in the passenger seat anymore but standing in the middle of the road in her nightie, waving frantically at me. I tried to hit the brakes, but I hit the accelerator instead and ploughed straight into her. The car veered off the road and landed in a lake, and as the vehicle was sinking, I banged on the doors and windscreen, trying to get out, but nothing would budge. Then I'd see Mum in the water in front of me, her long blonde hair floating upwards like tentacles as she tried to tell me something. Her lips were moving but nothing was coming out.

I woke up in a cold sweat at five a.m., sitting bolt upright in bed. Every time I had the dream it was so vivid it took me a while to realise it wasn't real when I came out of it.

I listened to the daytime sounds as my breathing calmed down again. The call of birds, an elephant trumpeting in the distance, the distant rumble of a Land Rover going out on an early morning game drive.

Richard and Jenna had stocked the fridge and cupboards with some essentials and I made a cup of tea, sitting on the veranda as the sun began to rise over the plains with a sweeping orange glow.

In a distant tree I saw the shape of a big cat, a leopard, I presumed, draped in the branches. There was nothing to stop it climbing down and rushing over to attack me. I remembered the lions bellowing last night and Richard's warning not to go into the bush alone. This place was dangerous. How could Dad bring me here? Would I be confined to the house and the lodge for the next year? Even though I'd made my house my prison in England, this would be far worse.

Despite the danger here, though, I was surprised to find that I wasn't scared. Maybe it was because it felt like this wasn't really happening. It seemed like I was just a spectator in my life. I was going through the motions, but I didn't feel like I was really here. Or maybe it was because there were far scarier things going on inside my head than out there. Nothing could be as bad as that.

'Jazz?' Dad called out an hour later with a worried tone.

'I'm out here.'

He opened the fly screen and his face relaxed with relief. 'I wondered where you were. Did you sleep OK?' He ran a hand through his rumpled hair.

'Not really. It's too noisy.' I didn't mention the dream. What was the point?

He ruffled my hair. 'Don't worry, you'll get used to it.' He sat down on the chair next to me. It creaked under his weight. Taking a deep breath of fresh air, he stared out across the wooden railings, the wrinkles around his eyes softening with an expression I hadn't seen in a long time. It was mixture of joy and relaxation. He looked like he'd just come home from a long, tiring journey.

A knife of guilt sliced through my chest. I was responsible for his unhappiness. I had to try harder to be nicer to him. I had to be a better daughter.

'Do you want to eat breakfast here or up at the lodge's kitchen before we go out on the game drive?' he said.

'Here, please.' I managed to raise a slight smile and he seemed pleased.

'You're going to love it here. I can feel it.' He stood up, stretched his arms over his head and said, 'Are scrambled eggs OK? There's some bread, too, if you want to rustle up some toast.'

Even though the thought of eating didn't appeal to me, I said, 'Eggs on toast sounds good.'

After breakfast I dressed in shorts and a T-shirt and rummaged around in my suitcases until I found a large sunhat with a wide brim that flopped over my face. I pulled it down low over my eyes and put on some big sunglasses. If I was lucky, no one would be able to see my face.

On the drive back to the lodge I relived in my mind what had happened last night in the kitchen. I didn't want to see Zach and the others again. As well as thinking I was abnormal, they probably thought I was crazy, too, and who wanted someone like that around?

The eggs churned in my stomach at the thought.

We entered the lodge's reception but there was no one around, so we made our way through to the garden and the pool area. Two pretty girls about eighteen years old were busy rubbing sun cream into their perfectly bronzed skin and laughing about something. One of them looked over at us and stared. From behind the safety of my sunglasses and hat I stared back at her. She had blonde straight hair like mine that hung down to her waist, but that was where the similarity ended. She had huge dark brown eyes, golden-tanned flawless skin, and a gym-toned figure. She was beautiful, and I felt a wave of jealousy wash over me.

She carried on blatantly staring and I lowered my head.

As Richard's voice called out to Dad from the bar area, I heard the girl say to her friend, 'Did you see that girl's face? Omigod, how could they leave her looking like that?'

Maybe my hat didn't cover as much of me as I'd hoped. I swallowed back the lump in my throat and shuffled close behind Dad.

Richard picked up a cool box and gave us a warm smile. 'Ready to go and see the reserve?'

'Absolutely.' Dad rubbed his hands together.

We headed off from the lodge in one of the Land Rovers, and I felt the wind whipping against my face, but it did little to relieve the heat pouring in through the open windows. The backs of my legs were dripping with sweat on the plastic seats before we'd even gone a mile. It felt like I'd been plunged into a bowl of boiling hot soup.

'Help yourselves to cold drinks in the cool box,' Richard shouted as we drove along a game path through a thicket of bushes and trees. 'Chef's packed us some sandwiches and fruit for lunch. We'll stop under some shade when it gets too hot and have a picnic.'

What, you mean it's going to get even hotter than this?

We drove past a herd of impala grazing on the short grasses, their rich red fur shimmering in the sun. They glanced up, seemingly undisturbed by our presence. Further on we saw some zebra and stopped to watch them for a while as they flicked their tails at the flies.

Miles later, we drove past a large watering hole and saw a crocodile, lazily basking on the banks, slyly watching a couple of small gazelles who had stopped for a much needed drink. Birds rested on top of their backs, pecking at the flies on their skin.

'Look, a cheetah!' Dad called out, pointing underneath a tree where the animal was lying down in a shady patch, licking its tail.

The cheetah got to its paws, stretched out its front legs and yawned, padding away with its tail swishing.

By lunchtime we hadn't even covered a quarter of the reserve, Richard told us as he drew the Land Rover to a stop beneath a large baobab tree. Dad grabbed the cool box and Richard set up some camp chairs under the shade of the branches.

'Ham salad or cheese and tomato?' Richard asked me, pulling out packets of sandwiches wrapped in greaseproof paper. 'Or maybe both? I think you need fattening up a bit. You're all skin and bones.' He smiled.

'Cheese, please.' I held out my hand and plonked myself down, grateful for the distraction of unwrapping the sandwich.

'There's a big lion pride in this area,' Richard said, sitting next to Dad. 'If we're lucky, we'll get to see them.'

'Have you had many problems with poachers here?' Dad asked.

'A little. Not as much as other places. We have six anti-poaching teams that patrol the reserve, but we need more. Trying to keep an eye on sixty-four square miles of land is a nightmare, especially at night.' He shook his head sadly. 'We've lost some animals. The tribe in the settlement further up say that some of the leopards and lions kill their goats and cattle, which is how they justify it, but, it's a load of rubbish.' He waved a hand through the air as if swatting a fly. 'Unless the fences are compromised, the animals can't get out, and we've never tracked any of the big cats near their settlement. Some of the locals are after buffalo, impala, and warthogs for food.' He took a bite of his sandwich, chewed and swallowed, then sat forward and carried on. 'Then there are the poachers who aren't local. They come for miles to get a leopard skin, or rhino horn, or ivory. They work for the big boys, the international animal traffickers. Some of the animal products are worth more than gold.' He shook his head angrily. 'A kilo of rhino horn is worth around fifty thousand dollars in China or Vietnam. They're even using leopard and lion bones in Chinese medicine now as a substitute for tigers because they've already wiped most of them out.' He pointed his fingers around the bush. 'We've lost three leopards in the last year to poachers, one rhino, two elephants, three lions, and one cheetah.' He shook his head solemnly. 'It's getting worse, Nathan.'

I drowned out their technical conversation and chewed on the sandwich, just for something to do.

When we finished lunch, we loaded everything back into the Land Rover and took off again. A couple of miles later, we spotted the lions. A huge male with a fluffy mane lay on his back under a bush, all four paws in the air. His belly was bloated with food. Six lionesses lay in various positions, eyes closed but ears twitching. One of them opened its eyes, raised its head and stared at us, then, seeing we weren't posing any danger, rested its head on its front paws and slid its eyelids shut. After ten minutes of sitting there watching them do not very much I grew restless in the sweaty seat.

'They're mostly active at night,' Dad said. 'They sleep most of the day away.'

I don't blame them.

'We've got a bull rhino around here we call Jimiyu,' Richard told Dad. 'I can see his tracks.' He pointed to some indents in the dusty ground. 'Let's see if we can follow him.'

A long and boring four hours later, we'd travelled through thick thorny scrub, shrubs, animal tracks, dirt roads, and woodlands, and seen lots of animals that Dad and Richard seemed pretty excited about. When we finally pulled up back at the game reserve I was ready for a cold shower. Make that two. Except, oh, yeah, there was no cold water.

'So, did you enjoy your first day here?' Dad draped an arm around me as we walked up the veranda steps after Richard dropped us off.

'Yes,' I lied.

One day down, three hundred and sixty-four more to go.

Chapter 5

I had another sleepless night, worrying about what the next day would bring working at the lodge. I was perfectly capable of cleaning my own bedroom and tidying up the house, since Mum always thought it taught me some 'responsibility.' But I didn't have a clue how to make a bed properly with all four corners tucked in to within a centimetre of their life. And on top of that, even though Richard and Jenna had been nice and friendly, I knew there were plenty of other people who wouldn't be. That girl by the pool, for starters. And what about Zach?

I shivered at the thought. There was just no getting away from the fact that people hated others who looked different to them. In the same way that people rubberneck at car accidents, they do it to people who look strange, too.

I dressed in the uniform that Jenna had sent over. A black skirt and blue short-sleeved blouse, black ballet-style shoes. I wanted to tie my hair up away from my face to try and cool my neck down but there was no chance of that. It would stay down, hiding as much as was possible.

I refused breakfast when Dad offered. There was no way I was going to keep anything down. And with shaking hands, I got into the Land Rover with Dad and we drove to the lodge.

'Morning!' Jenna called out cheerily from behind the reception desk. Bobo looked up and I swear I saw a smile on her face. 'I hope you enjoyed your tour yesterday,' Jenna went on. 'Now the real work begins. Don't worry, we'll take good care of Jazz.' She glanced at Dad. 'Have a great first day.'

He grinned back, itching with excitement to pick up some medical supplies and head off with Richard to the other side of the reserve, where they'd had a report from one of the rangers about an injured gazelle.

'Good luck, Jazz.' He gave me a thumbs-up before heading off.

Jenna led me past the guests eating breakfast in the dining room. Their relaxed conversation and tinkling laughter carried through the hot air. I kept my head firmly down, concentrating on the path in front of me, not wanting to bump into those two girls again.

'Fathiya is in the store room sorting out the laundry for the guest rooms,' Jenna said, hurrying towards the back of the main lodge building. She led the way into a large storeroom, packed with sheets, towels, cleaning supplies, and complimentary bottles of toiletries.

A short, very round black woman leaned over the lowest shelf with her back to us, scooping up armfuls of sheets.

'Morning, Fathiya!' Jenna sing-songed.

'Morning, Miss Jenna.' She turned around and gave her a toothy smile.

Fathiya was probably in her fifties with hair so short it was almost shaved. Her gaze moved from Jenna's face to mine and the smile dropped. She put the sheets onto a nearby trolley loaded high with bedding and cupped either side of my face in her hands with a strong grip, lifting my head up to the light. Then she started chuckling. A sound which was like a big, booming, 'Hunh, hunh, hunh.'

'Child, you look like a long lost African girl,' she said.

I tried to pull away but her grip was too strong.

I didn't have a clue what she was talking about as she peered intensely into my eyes. How could I be an African girl? I was as white as an iceberg.

'You sure you're not from the Kikuyu tribe?' She cackled. 'Hunh, hunh, hunh.'

Luckily, she released her grip then and I pulled away, hot with embarrassment, moving out of grabbing distance.

'Now, Fathiya, don't frighten the poor girl,' Jenna scolded her gently, realising that it was very uncomfortable for me.

Jenna gave Fathiya a look, as if to say, *I've warned you, she doesn't like attention.*

Fathiya threw her head back and laughed again, waving a dismissive hand through the air. 'Jazz is just fine, aren't you, child?'

I didn't utter a word. I was far from fine. No one had ever blatantly just grabbed me and stared at my face before. I felt nauseous, and I didn't know how I was going to get through an hour of working with her, let alone a whole day.

'Show her what she needs to do, Fathiya, and I'll catch up with you both later on.'

'We'll be fine, Miss Jenna.'

Jenna nodded at us and disappeared, and I was left standing there uncomfortably, wishing I'd never set foot in this horrible country.

'Follow me, Jazz.' Fathiya gave me another toothy smile and pushed the trolley out of the door. 'Miss Jenna and Mr Richard are lovely to work for. They are good people. There aren't many jobs around this area, but the game reserve pays us enough to feed our family. You make sure you do a good job for them.' She nodded.

The first bedroom we went into was pretty tidy. Fathiya chatted incessantly, telling me about her family of five children and the settlement she lived in as she supervised me tidying, dusting, vacuuming, and cleaning the en suite bathroom. Luckily, she didn't ask me anything about myself and was happy just to talk.

'Do you know how to make a bed properly?' she asked, bringing in sheets from the trolley positioned outside the door after we'd stripped the bed.

I shook my head.

'Hunh, hunh, hunh. It's easy. We want the guests to think they're sleeping on a cloud!' She grabbed a sheet by two corners, and with a practiced flick of her wrists, she threw the ends over the bed. It landed almost perfectly.

I watched her work the corners over the bed so it was smooth and flat. 'Your turn.' She nodded encouragingly to my side of the bed, but however hard I tried, I just couldn't get the same result. My fringe stuck to my forehead with sweat, and I could feel my shirt clinging to my back as I tugged and tucked, pulled it out and redid it numerous times. I could feel the frustration and anger simmering up to the surface.

This is ridiculous! What am I doing here? I'm never going to get the hang of this, and I don't even want to.

'Here, like this.' She came round to my side and patiently showed me again.

Defeated, I let her finish it, and she gave one last satisfied glance round the room before we left.

The next room looked like a bomb had gone off. There was a suitcase on the floor and designer clothes strewn around every available surface. Makeup and toiletries lined the bathroom shelf haphazardly, and the bedclothes were hanging on the floor, but Fathiya didn't bat an eyelid. Maybe she'd seen worse.

Fathiya decided she would clean the bathroom and asked me to try making the bed on my own. As I was tugging and pulling the sheets on the bed again, the door opened.

My head instinctively swung round to the door and I found myself looking at the blonde-haired girl from the pool.

'Oh!' Her eyes widened and her forehead wrinkled in a frown of distaste as she stared at me.

I quickly bent my head and busied myself attacking the sheet while her dark-haired friend walked in.

'I hope you don't think I'm sleeping on that!' The blonde-haired girl scowled, pointing to the bed where the sheets were ruffled and wonky, and looking like a complete mess.

My hands shook as I wiped the sweat off my forehead with the back of my hand and carried on attempting to put the top sheet on, but however hard I tried I just couldn't get it straight.

'Hello?' she sneered. 'Are you deaf as well?'

'Sorry,' I mumbled. 'I'm trying to fix it.'

'Urgh! And now you're sweating all over the sheets. It's

disgusting.' She stalked up to me and said, 'Get out of here. I don't want you in my room. I might catch something.'

Hearing all the commotion, Fathiya came out of the bathroom. 'Is everything all right, miss?' she asked the girl as her dark-haired friend gave me a haughty stare.

The blonde girl stood, one hand on her hip, one hand pointing at me, glaring in my direction. 'No, it most certainly is not all right. Wait until Daddy hears about this. He won't be very happy to have this...this weirdo touching my things!'

Everything just seemed to snap in me then. I could feel a tsunami of energy exploding its way to the surface. The accident. Mum. My injuries. Being in Africa. Being made fun of all the time. The injustice of it all. It was just too much.

I heard a groaning sound, like the cry from a wounded animal, and I realised it was coming from me. I flung the pillow I was holding onto the bed with such force it bounced onto the floor and I ran out of the room.

Storming up the path, head down, I felt angry hot tears running down my cheeks. I intended to walk back to our quarters but a pair of legs blocked my path.

I heard Zach's voice say, 'Hey, what's the rush?' I felt his hands on my shoulders. 'Are you OK?'

My shoulders crumpled and I let the sobs overtake me. 'I...I...' But I couldn't get the words out.

How could he possibly understand the depths of pain and loneliness in my world? I bet everything was just rosy in his life. I pushed past him and ran up the path and around the back of the lodge towards our house.

When I got there, I didn't know what to do. I paced the veranda, willing myself to calm down. I couldn't do this job. It was too soon to be around all these people. I just wanted to go back home and hibernate for the rest of my life. Pull the covers over my head and never get out of bed again.

I took a deep breath and sniffed, wiping away the tears. It was hopeless. Everything was hopeless.

I ran out of the house, forgetting the warnings of Richard and Dad not to go out into the bush on my own. The wind whistled in my ears as I sprinted towards a tall outcrop of rocks that I'd seen when we went for our drive the day before. In my old life, I'd spent hours at the local leisure centre's climbing wall and later joined a climbing club, travelling all over the country in pursuit of the next great rocks to master. It always seemed to clear my head. It gave me a sense of strength and freedom. That's what I needed now, freedom.

I was out of breath when I arrived, but that didn't stop me. I took my first foothold on the grey rocks and began my climb, a smooth rhythm of fingers and toes working over the crevices and cracks. I'd stopped climbing after the accident, but now it was like I'd never been away from it. My mind emptied of thoughts. All I could hear was my breath. In. Out. In. Out. My own personal meditation space. When I reached the top my arms were shaking from being out of practice. I sat on top of the rocks and stared out at the horizon.

What the hell was I going to do? I knew Dad thought he was helping me by bringing me here, but it wasn't working. It had just made things so much worse.

'Mum, what am I going to do?' I cried out in despair. 'Please help me.'

I sat there, knees bent close to my chest with my head resting on them, for a long time, worrying what Dad was going to say. I didn't want to spoil things for him, but I just couldn't cope with this.

As the thoughts tumbled around in my brain, I heard a noise and jerked my head up, suddenly hearing Richard's warning come into my head. I was out here alone, in the middle of Africa with wild animals and snakes.

I strained my ears, listening to the noise. It sounded like a cry. A high-pitched squeaky cry, like an animal in distress. I stood up and walked to the edge of the rocks, looking down. At the bottom I saw a tiny leopard cub with huge blue eyes, looking up at me and mewing as its little legs tried to get a foothold at the bottom of the rocks.

It was so thin its shoulder blades were almost poking through the skin. The desperation in its pitiful wail seemed to permeate right through to my bones, and my first thought was to climb down and soothe it. My second thought was that wherever there was a baby leopard, there would be a mother leopard, and even though I didn't particularly value my own life anymore, I didn't really want to die painfully by being mauled and scratched to death.

I willed it to shut up so it wouldn't attract its mother's attention, or maybe the attention of scavenging hyenas that Dad had said could crack bone with their jaws. I didn't know if hyenas could climb rocks, but the mother leopard definitely could. I moved away from the edge so the cub was out of my sight and pressed my hands over my ears, trying to drown out the helpless sound.

When it didn't work, I leaned over the edge of the rocks again and flapped my hands in the air. 'Go away!' I yelled down.

That didn't work, either. In fact, my voice, or the sight of me, seemed to make it worse, and the distressed sounds got louder.

I looked up at the sky and exhaled. What was I supposed to do?

I looked down into the cub's big blue eyes and it stared back. No, maybe that was wrong. It seemed like it was actually seeing through me. Right into my soul, like it knew me, the real Jazz. Not the the ugly, scarred Jazz. And since the accident, no one had ever done that.

I felt something strange happening. I can't explain it, really, and it sounds stupid to even try, but I felt an overwhelming connection with this helpless creature sweep over me, right through my heart. You know how, when you listen to a meaningful song that grips at your core and gives you goosebumps, it's like that song was written only for you? That's how it was with the cub. There had to be a reason it was here at these rocks.

I thought back to Mum's firm belief that everything happened for a reason. Had she just answered my cries? Does that sound pathetic, like I was grasping at straws? Maybe it was pathetic, but for the first time since the accident I was actually feeling something other than pain and fear and sadness, and I couldn't explain it.

For some reason, this cub needed me, and when I peered over the opposite side of the rocks I thought I knew the reason why.

Blood. There were lots of dark brownish-red stains on the ground with flies buzzing around and drag marks leading away into the trees beyond. And that's when it hit me in the chest with the force of a punch.

This cub had lost her mother. This cub was just like me.

Chapter 6

I climbed quickly down the rocks, all fear of being attacked by animals vanishing from my thoughts. I wondered how long the cub had been left on its own. It must've been a while since it was obviously starving and practically skin and bone. If I didn't get it back to Dad as quickly as possible it could die.

When I got to the bottom, the cub reached up and let me scoop it into my arms. It stopped crying and sucked on my fingertips urgently, searching for milk, abandoning one and moving onto the next one when it realised it couldn't get what it wanted. I held the cub close to me as I hurried through the bush, stroking its soft fur and talking in a gentle voice to try and reassure it. All the way back it kept my fingertip in its mouth and fixed its huge eyes on my face.

There was a radio in our quarters. I had to try and get hold of Dad. He'd know what to do. Bursting in through the front door, I grabbed the radio from its charger unit and sat at the kitchen table with the cub on my lap.

I pressed a button on the side and called out, 'Dad! Dad, are you there?'

Crackly static came over the air.

'Dad! Dad, answer me.'

'Jazz?' Dad said. 'Is that you?'

'I need you back at the house,' I cried.

'What's happened? Are you all right?'

'Yes, but I've found an injured animal and I need you to come back right away.'

'What? The reception's not very good here. What have you found?'

'Just come back to the house! There's an animal that needs

your help.'

'I'm leaving now. I'll be there in about fifteen minutes. Stay there.'

I put the radio on the table and stared at the cub lying on its back in my lap, showing me its soft belly. I stoked its head as it stared back.

What had I just done? What if its mum wasn't dead? Was I just being stupid, imagining that it needed me? I didn't know hardly anything about wild animals. I'd never been really interested before, not like Mum and Dad. But then what about the blood? There was loads of it. Surely a leopard couldn't have survived that much blood loss. Hadn't Richard been talking about poachers who were after leopards the day before? I wracked my brains, trying to think of what he'd said, but I hadn't been listening at the time and couldn't remember much.

By the time I heard Dad pull up in the Land Rover the cub was in a peaceful sleep with one of my fingertips in its mouth.

He rushed through the front door calling out, 'Jazz? Are you OK?' He flew into the kitchen and stopped abruptly, staring at the baby leopard.

His jaw dropped, anger and worry mixed into one written all over his face. 'How on earth did you get hold of a leopard cub?' He picked it up from my lap and put it on the table, going into vet mode and giving it a thorough examination. The instant it was removed from my lap, the cub started mewing again, turning its head towards me and wriggling to get back.

'Jazz, where did you find it?' he asked sternly, his hands feeling over the bones and muscles, his fingertips prising its eyelids open, and looking in its mouth.

'It was at the bottom of those big rocks we drove past yesterday.'

He stopped his examination and his head snapped up, eyes flashing. 'What did Richard and I tell you about not going off on your own? Anything could've happened. What if its mother had come back? You wouldn't have stood a chance with an angry mother leopard.'

I told him about the blood and the drag marks.

'You don't know the blood came from its mother. It could've been from an animal its mother had killed and eaten. It could've been prey killed by a lion. What were you thinking?' His voice rose.

He was right. I didn't know. It just felt like the right thing to do.

The cub's mewing grew stronger as it struggled to get back to me. I reached out my hand and stroked its head, which instantly quietened it down.

'Why were you even out there? You're supposed to be working at the lodge.'

'I'm not going back there, Dad, I can't. I can't face people being mean to me. One of the guests called me a weirdo.'

His eyebrows furrowed in surprise. 'Why would they do that?'

I pointed to my face. 'Look at me! I *am* a weirdo.' I carried on stroking the cub and changed the subject. 'Is it OK?'

'It's a she, and yes, she's OK. Dehydrated and starving, but she looks OK.' He shook his head. 'You're sure there was blood?'

I nodded firmly. 'I may be a weirdo freak, but I know blood when I see it.'

He grabbed the radio on his belt and pressed the button. 'Richard, come in, Richard.'

'Receiving,' Richard replied. 'Go ahead.'

'Jazz has found a leopard cub near the outcrop and apparently there's a lot of blood and some drag marks nearby. Can you meet me there? I'm going to check it out. We may have an injured mother out there, or possible poachers.'

'I'll see you there in five,' he replied.

Dad pointed his finger at me. 'I'll mix up some milk formula for her when I get back, if we don't find her mother.

Do not move!'

I picked up the cub and she wasted no time getting settled in my lap, gently sucking on my fingertips again before falling into a twitchy sleep.

I studied her carefully. The dark rosette spots on her coat, her fine eyelashes and whiskers. She had huge paws and a gangly body with a tiny head and ears, but she was the most beautiful creature I'd ever seen. No matter what Dad said, I just knew her mother was dead, and I wanted to keep her. She'd been prised away from all the safety and love she'd ever known, and I had to do everything I could to protect her, to give her the life her mother couldn't anymore.

An hour later, Dad returned. Seeing me in the same position as when he'd left, he sat down wearily at the kitchen table and looked between me and the cub.

'Well?' I prompted. 'Did you find the mum?'

He exhaled a deep breath and shook his head. 'Richard and his trackers have been scouring the area. They found the markings of an adult female leopard interspersed with the blood and tracks of poachers. They're following the poachers' trail now to see if they can catch them, but it's pretty certain that her mother has been killed.'

The cub whimpered in her sleep, as if somehow realising what Dad had said. I looked down at her and then back to Dad.

'I want to keep her,' I said firmly.

He stood up again. 'I'm going to mix her some milk formula from the office and I'll be back in about ten minutes. We'll talk then.'

As Dad left, she stretched her paws in the air and blinked her eyes open, looking deep into mine as if to say, *Thank you for saving me*.

'I don't care what he says, I'm keeping you.' I smiled at her, my facial muscles stretching in an unfamiliar expression.

She nudged her head against my hand in reply and turned over, padding her front paws on my knees like she'd do to her mum to stimulate milk.

'I'll give you some in a minute when Dad gets back.' I giggled as her paws tickled my skin.

'Well, I haven't heard that sound in a long time.' Dad stood, observing me carefully from the doorway with a half-smile on his face and a baby's bottle full of milk in one hand.

He approached us and knelt down in front of the cub, tipping up the bottle and squeezing a couple of drips onto his finger. He slowly reached his finger towards her so she could smell the milk. Even though she must've been dying to drink, she pulled her head away from him. He tried repeatedly to coax her to lick his finger but she wasn't having any of it, moving closer to me and burying her head in the crook of my arm.

'If she doesn't take it, she's not going to last very long.' He held the bottle out. 'You try.'

I dripped some of the formula onto my finger and held it close to her face.

Please take it.

She slowly looked up at me, then looked at my finger.

Come on, take it, little girl.

Carefully, she licked off the few drops then looked around for more. I tipped the bottle upside down and she licked that, too, then sucked hard, her front paws clutching around my fingers as I held the bottle for her. She fed hungrily, gazing into my eyes all the time.

'She likes you,' Dad said, sitting down at the table next to me.

'I want to keep her.' I stroked her back with my other hand while she suckled.

'You can't keep a leopard as a pet. She's a wild animal.'

'But she's lost her mum. I know how that feels. She needs someone to look after her. At least until she's old enough to look after herself. Please, Dad.'

Dad's forehead pinched into a frown and he stared at the table, thinking. 'And then what? Release her into the wild? It wouldn't work. She wouldn't have any of the attributes she'd need to survive on her own that she'd normally learn from her mother. A cat's behaviour depends on genetics, intuition, and individual learning. She may have natural instincts to hunt but she needs the skill taught by her mother. Plus, she'd be so used to humans it would be dangerous for her.'

'They did it with the lion Elsa from *Born Free*. I saw the film,' I said stubbornly.

'Elsa died,' he said flatly.

'That wasn't their fault. There must be a way,' I pleaded.

'It's only ever been done a few times before with a leopard cub,' Zach's voice interrupted us as he stood in the doorway to the kitchen, arms folded, leaning against the door frame.

I'd been so intent on trying to convince Dad that I hadn't even heard him come in.

I looked up at him and our eyes locked for a second before he swept his gaze to the cub.

'It's not easy to re-wild a big cat like this to release back into the wild,' Zach said, sitting down opposite me.

'But if it's been done before, even a couple of times, it could work, couldn't it?' I said to Zach. If I could convince him, maybe I could convince Dad to let me try, too.

'Your dad's right, though,' Zach replied. 'If she gets too friendly with humans, she could be in danger from poachers. Or the opposite, which sometimes happens with cats who've gone through re-wilding, is that they don't fear humans anymore, so if they approach a human who then runs, it triggers their hunting instinct and they attack them.' He tilted his head, looking slowly between me and the cub.

I looked down at the little bundle of fur contentedly sucking and dismissed the idea she'd ever do anything like that.

'Exactly,' Dad agreed.

'So what do you want to do? Kill her now? Send her to a zoo?' My eyes blazed at them both as I thought of her pacing in front of a cage with glazed, vacant eyes, having retreated so deep into herself to try and survive the desolation of captivity. 'Don't you want to even give her a chance?'

'There's a lot of controversy trying to train these types of animals for release into the wild.' Dad rested his elbows on the table and rubbed his fingertips over his forehead.

'I could do it,' I said to them both. 'I'll learn.'

'It's not like you can just start something like this and then give up when things go wrong.' Zach leaned back in the chair and folded his arms, eyes coolly appraising me. 'There are hundreds of things that could affect her chances.'

I held on to his gaze with determination. 'I'll do whatever it takes. She deserves to grow up and be out there where she belongs.' I jerked my head towards the window.

Dad studied me for a while and then said to Zach, 'Can I have a word with you outside?'

That's right, just talk about me behind my back.

I glared at their backs as they disappeared outside onto the veranda.

I heard snippets of conversation through the open window...

Dad: '...the first time I've seen a spark of interest in her since the accident...'

Zach: '...endangered animals. We need more leopards in the wild to prevent them becoming wiped out...'

Dad: '...don't think it can be done...'

Zach: '...low success rate...'

Dad: '...I've tried everything I can think of with her...'

Zach: '...maybe it will help her move on...'

Dad: '...it trusts her...'

Eventually, they returned and sat down at the table. Zach tilted his head to the ceiling and avoided my questioning look. Dad looked at the cub that had finished the whole bottle and was now sucking my finger and hiccupping after guzzling her milk so hard. My heart just melted at her vulnerability, and I could feel my throat constricting with the fear that they were going to say no.

'You're going to have to work closely with Zach on this,'

Dad said to me. 'It's going to take a lot of effort and determination if there's even going to be a chance of this thing working.'

'I think she's about eight weeks old,' Zach said. 'It will take nearly two years before she's ready to be released, and that's a huge commitment. You can't bail out at the first sign of any problems. This is an animal's life we're talking about here, and it's not something to take on lightly.'

I sat upright in my chair. 'I don't care. I'll do it. I'll do whatever it takes.'

'And there's one condition.' Zach's cool topaz gaze met mine from across the table.

'What's that?' I asked.

'We should film it for a documentary.'

I furrowed my eyebrows together. 'A documentary?'

He nodded.

'Didn't you know Richard's a wildlife filmmaker?' Dad said.

I shook my head.

'He's filmed lots of pieces for National Geographic. Even worked with David Attenborough,' Zach told me. 'But he wouldn't be filming it. I would.' He glanced down at the cub. 'She obviously trusts you, and I think it would be dangerous to the outcome if she got too close to too many people, so you would have the primary role in re-wilding her.' He leaned forward, making sure I was taking it in. 'It would involve filming you working with the cub. It would make a great documentary and would have a conservation message about anti-poaching.'

'S...so I'd have to be on film, too?' I looked to Dad for help.

Dad nodded.

'But...I...I...' I couldn't get the words out. I felt like they'd given me the greatest gift and taken it away again in the same breath. How could I be on film for the whole world to see and laugh at? It would be my worst nightmare.

Zach stood up to leave. 'That's the deal. These cats are

poached for their fur and bones. They're used in tribal ceremonies, fashion, and medicine. If we don't do something to stop the killing, they'll become extinct. A documentary is one way we can get the message out there.'

I looked down at the cub and had that overwhelming feeling again that this was supposed to happen, that she'd purposely found me on that rock. As if to show her agreement, she stretched up on her hind legs, lifted her front paws up to me and gently placed them on either side of my face. This was about something far bigger than my feelings.

'OK, OK, I'll do it,' I said breathlessly before they changed their minds.

Zach sat back down, the ghost of a grin on his lips. 'Good. Well, if we're going to do this, we need to think of a name for her.'

'A name,' I repeated, thinking. What did you call an African leopard? Somehow I didn't think Fluffy or Spotty would be appropriate. It needed to be something special.

'How about Asha?' Zach said. 'It means *life* in Swahili. If you pull this off, you'll be giving her back her life.'

I rolled the name around my tongue. 'Asha.' It was perfect. I smiled back at him. 'I love it.'

Zach stood once again and held his hand out for me to shake. 'Then we have a deal.'

He took my limp hand in his firm grip, calmly appraising me as we shook on it.

It wasn't until he'd left I realised that, apart from Dad and Katrina, he was the first person I'd looked square in the eyes since the accident. For a few moments, I'd completely forgotten about my face.

Chapter 7

After Zach left, Dad leaned back in his chair, looking between me and Asha, his lips pressed together in a pensive line.

'Are you sure you're up to this?' he asked me gently.

I glanced down at Asha in my lap as she lay on her back, her eyes half closed but still never wavering from my face. I nodded firmly at Dad. I was more sure of it than anything. How could I let her live the rest of her life in a zoo? It would be a prison, and I knew all about living in those.

'I'm positive,' I said.

He studied me for a long time and then rubbed his hands on his trousers. 'Well, then.' He got to his feet. 'Looks like I'd better bring the rest of that formula in from the Land Rover.'

After lugging in plastic baby bottles, milk powder, and tubs of various other vitamins and calcium supplements that he said she'd need, he left it all on the kitchen table.

'She's going to need feeding every two hours at the moment,' he said, showing me how to mix up the formula and add the other nutrients. 'Have you got any questions before I get back to work? We've got a lion being brought in today from the Masai Mara area for re-release here. Apparently, it's been attacking the Masai cattle and they want to establish it somewhere else before it gets shot, so I need to get going. It's all hands on deck.'

'I'm fine,' I said. 'I've got the radio if I need to contact you.'

He kissed me on the top of the head. 'Well, make sure you do that. And don't go wandering off in the bush again, especially with her. If she gets lost, she won't survive.'

After he left, I spent the afternoon getting to know Asha and showing her round the house. She ignored most of it and seemed content to follow me everywhere as I chatted to her in a soft voice. She'd let me know if she wanted a cuddle by mewing at me, although the desperation I'd heard in her voice earlier had gone now. After feeding her, I realised that there could be a potential potty training problem when she weed on the wooden floorboards in the kitchen, so from then on, after she'd had her feed, I took her outside and sat on the steps, putting her gently down onto the parched soil and rubbing her belly so she would hopefully go to the toilet. She learned quickly, and after the third time she seemed to get the hang of it.

The hazy light of the fading day was settling on the horizon when Dad arrived back and found me dozing in a hammock on the veranda with little Asha tucked into the crook of my arm, her head resting on my stomach.

'Looks like you've had a busy day,' he said, taking off his hat and wiping his forehead with the back of his hand.

'It was great.' I grinned back at him, chatting incessantly like a proud parent about how Asha had taken all of her feed, had her first potty-trained wee, and behaved like the perfect child.

I picked Asha up and set her down on the floor as we walked into the kitchen. She followed so close behind me I felt her whiskers on the back of my legs. 'How was the lion release? Did everything go OK?' I asked.

'It went perfectly. Hopefully he'll have a couple of new girlfriends before long. We've got too many lionesses here at the moment and not enough males. I think he's going to be a lucky boy!' He looked in the fridge and pulled out an onion, some peppers, a tomato, and some eggs. 'Do you fancy an omelette for dinner?'

I realised then that I was starving. All this being on constant alert to make sure Asha was OK and not getting into mischief was making me hungry. 'I'd love one.'

He got to work on the omelette and I heard a knock at the

door. I glanced questioningly at Dad.

'That will be Zach,' he said.

'Zach? Why?' I whispered, my heartbeat dancing around as I remembered trying to eat in front of him at the lodge and the disastrous water incident.

'Because you two are going to be working closely with each other on this and you need to get to know each other,' he whispered back, then called out to Zach, 'Come in. We're in the kitchen.'

Zach appeared in the doorway, looking fresh and clean, his hair damp from a recent shower. I could smell a mixture of outdoors and something fragrant. It wasn't until he spoke that I realised I was staring at his lips.

I quickly looked down to the floor at Asha who was standing on her hind legs, begging to be picked up.

'Come and sit down.' Dad nodded his head to the table, then dished up two plates of the omelette. 'Tuck in,' he said to us.

'Aren't you eating?' I asked, noticing that he hadn't got anything for himself.

'Oh, didn't I mention it? I'm eating up at the lodge. I've got a few exciting ideas about a possible rhino breeding programme I want to talk over with Richard.' He patted us both on the shoulder and said, 'Won't be long.'

I stared at the food on my plate.

Zach picked up his fork and popped a piece into his mouth. 'Aren't you hungry?'

I could feel the weight of his gaze on my face and I felt a red rash of embarrassment creeping up my neck.

'How's Asha been?' He shifted in his chair so he could get a better look at her where she'd settled under the table, playing with the laces on my walking boots.

'She's been very well behaved.' I stole a tentative look at him from underneath my fringe as he concentrated on Asha. Satisfied he wasn't looking at me, I picked up my fork and slowly swallowed a mouthful of food. And before I knew it, I'd filled him in on Asha's day and the food had disappeared.

He pushed his plate away and leaned back in the chair. 'We need to talk about a plan for her.'

'What sort of a plan?' I stood up and deposited the plates in the sink, turning my back to him. Asha followed me and continued to play with my laces as I made up her formula.

'If this is going to work, you're going to essentially be her mum for the next two years. That means you'll have to play with her to hone her natural hunting instincts, then eventually teach her to hunt. You'll have to exercise her daily to build up her strength, show her the area that's going to be her home, teach her to climb.'

Well, at least I knew how to do one of those things well. I sat down at the table again, deposited Asha on my lap and let her suck greedily from the bottle. 'I understand that.'

'She can't live in the house forever, she's not a pet. When she's about four months old her mum would naturally introduce her to feeding on her kills so we have to feed her with carcasses.' I felt his cool eyes on me, making sure I was taking this all in.

Carcasses? Dead animals? The omelette suddenly wasn't sitting very well in my stomach.

'I hope you're not squeamish because you'll have to feed her,' he said.

I glanced up sharply. 'Me? Can't you feed them to her?'

He shook his head. 'Like I said, you're her mum. You have to be able to do everything she would for her.' He paused, letting it sink in. 'Can you do that? Because you can't just start this and then back out a few months down the line. I'm trying to prepare you for what will happen if it all goes to plan.'

The thought of having to haul around dead animals to feed her was disgusting, but then, what did I think I was going to feed her? Industrial-sized tins of Kitty Kat? In fact, I hadn't thought about it. I hadn't thought about the seriousness of the situation until then. But one thing I did know was that I was going to do everything in my power to make sure she was released back into the reserve with a fighting chance of survival.

'There will come a time when we have to introduce her to live prey and teach her to hunt for herself,' he went on.

'How can you watch that, though?' I asked. 'One animal tearing another to pieces.'

'It's the law of nature, Jazz.' He shrugged. 'There will always be animals that are predators and those that are prey. It keeps an equal balance. It's not something you can ever change.' He rested his elbows on the table and leaned forwards. 'We'll need to build an enclosure for her somewhere nearby. I've seen a good spot just outside that I think would work.'

I stroked Asha's soft underbelly as he spoke. When she finished suckling, I put her back down on the floor.

'Sorry, I need to take her for a toilet run.' I walked towards the front door, calling Asha's name and she obediently followed me as Zach brought up the rear.

I sat down on the steps and Zach sat next to me. We both watched her sniffing the ground, maybe seeing if it was a good spot to do her toilet duties. His thighs were so close to mine, I could feel the heat from his body radiating out into my skin. I shuffled away slightly. There was no way I wanted him catching a look at my face in this close proximity.

'And, of course, I'll be filming the whole thing,' he said.

I swallowed back the lump in my throat and nodded. I'd make sure that I wore my hat pulled down low over my face.

He stood up, walked to his Land Rover and opened the door. When he came back he carried a rubber tyre and a long stick with a piece of rope tied to the end. 'Toys.' He held them out. 'Some people think that wild predators have a natural hunting instinct and some think it's learned from their mothers. I think it's a bit of both, but playing helps that instinct to come out. It's something they'd do in the wild and it will build her strength up, too.'

He put the tyre on the ground and I took the stick, holding

it in my hand and dangling the rope in front of Asha, swishing it from side to side. She looked cross-eyed as she tried to focus on it, her paws sweeping in the air in front of her in a very uncoordinated way. At least it might save my laces from annihilation.

'We'll need to take her for walks every morning and afternoon to build her strength up,' he said, watching Asha. 'Small ones at first, then gradually longer and longer.'

'OK.' I laughed when she reached up to the rope and fell onto her back.

I heard him chuckle next to me and watched out of the corner of my eye as he turned his head towards me. 'What happened back at the lodge this morning?' he said softly.

I felt my stomach muscles clench and turned my head away from his, looking out at the fading sunset of oranges, reds, and yellows slicing through the sky. If I told him, would he laugh at me like all the other people had at school? Would he make a horrible comment and point out that I deserved it?

And then from nowhere, I felt this sudden urge to tell him what had happened. I hadn't talked to anyone in a long time. Not really talked. All these feelings and thoughts I'd bottled up inside seemed to spill to the surface.

I opened my mouth. Closed it. Took a deep breath. 'There are a couple of girls staying at the lodge and they were mean to me,' I finally said, still staring at the sky disappearing into darkness. 'They called me things.' I held my breath, waiting for the cutting remark or the laugh of ridicule.

'Just because someone says something, it doesn't mean it's true. There are always going to be people who think they're better than you,' he said. 'You're never going to change that. But you're the only one who has power over your thoughts. It doesn't matter what they think. The only thing that's important is what *you* think.'

Chapter 8

It felt like I only managed to snatch a few hours sleep every night. I set my alarm clock to get up and feed Asha regularly, and what with the time spent suckling on the bottle and outside toilet duties, it seemed like I'd no sooner got to sleep than I was up again, ready to start the next round. I tried to settle Asha down on a few blankets next to my bed, but she cried and cried until I lifted her onto the bed next to me and she quickly snuggled up to any available patch of skin.

The days settled into an easy routine. Zach arrived twice a day at six a.m. and around five p.m. in between his game ranger duties, and we took a short walk through the bush with Asha on a lead. She had a bright-eyed curiosity about everything, chasing beetles, flies, and anything that seemed to move, practising her hunting skills for later life. Lizards were a particular favourite of hers, but all the insects and reptiles made strange noises for her to investigate. I was very conscious of Zach filming me and little Asha as we took in the sights of the reserve. There were many times when the brim of my hat was so low over my face that I didn't see fallen branches or rocks until it was too late and ended up tripping over them, nearly dying of embarrassment.

'Take your hat off,' he said one day while he filmed us from a little way behind. 'You're going to hurt yourself.'

I shook my head. No way. I still couldn't believe I'd even agreed to be on camera at all, but then, I had no choice. Not if I wanted to do what was best for Asha.

'Have you lived here all your life?' I asked, trying to change the subject.

He turned the camera off and caught up with me. 'As soon

as I was old enough to walk this bush became my playground. When I was growing up, Dad took me everywhere. He'd spend hours filming the wildlife, and his love for Africa was infectious. There's nothing like it on earth, and I could never imagine being anywhere else.'

We wandered down towards the river that snaked through the reserve, and I felt his hand grab my arm, stopping me in my tracks.

He pointed to a huge black snake in our path. 'It's a black mamba.'

I launched myself onto Zach with fright, my arms latched round his neck and my knees shaking.

Asha instinctively froze, staring at the snake with a suspicious frown crinkled on her face.

The snake reared up its head, hissing.

'Don't move.' He held me round the waist firmly. 'It's the most poisonous snake in Africa. They're normally shy, but if they feel cornered they can get pretty aggressive.'

I felt my heartbeat banging hard, threatening to explode. I took hold of Asha's collar in case she got a stupid idea to try and investigate it.

'Back up a bit.' He clutched me tight into his body as we stepped back slowly.

I watched, shaking, as the snake gave us one last look and slithered away. I finally allowed myself to breathe again.

Zach released his arm.

'You OK?' he asked.

I nodded warily. 'I've never been that close to a dangerous snake before.'

'You always have to be alert out here. You never know what you're going to come across round the next corner.' He patted his rifle slung over one shoulder. 'This comes in handy to fire warning shots in case something gets out of hand.'

We waited until the snake had well and truly disappeared before I released Asha and we carried on to the river. A gazelle stood with its feet in the shallows as it stood drinking, looking up skittishly every now and then to search for possible danger. I spied a large monitor lizard busy sunning itself on the rocks and keeping a beady eye on the dragonflies hovering over the water. It was oblivious to a jackal silently creeping up behind it.

I wondered who would get their prize first, the lizard or the jackal. The gazelle barked out an alarm that sent the lizard scuttling for cover. It looked like neither of them would get their breakfast.

We sat on the banks of the river and Asha put her front legs in the water and then dashed back out again, shaking her paws and staring at them in wonder. Backwards and forwards she went until she plucked up enough courage to stand with all four paws in. Then she couldn't get enough of it, splashing around to her heart's content, pawing at fish under the surface.

'So, you're not used to snakes, huh?' Zach said.

'No.'

'I bet with your mum and dad being so obsessed with animals you must've had some weird and wonderful pets, though.'

I gazed at the shimmering water. 'Well, Mum was always bringing home waifs and strays from her job as a veterinary nurse, but I kind of left her to it. I wasn't really in to animals.'

His eyes widened and he gave me an odd look, as if I'd just told him that the clouds rained chocolate. 'Not into animals?' He shook his head softly. 'Wow, you've missed out on a lot.'

I shrugged. Maybe it was because my parents were both so obsessed with animals that I was jealous of all the ones my mum brought home, and I always felt like Dad abandoned us, really. He spent so much time at the safari park, he was hardly at home when I was growing up. But now things had changed. If this was going to be Asha's world then I wanted to know everything about it so I could prepare her for life out here in the bush.

'I want you to teach me about this place and the animals,' I said, looking at the jackal who had reappeared, trying to sniff out the lizard.

'I can teach you, but it's easier to show you, and that will take a long time. It's a bit different from England, eh?' He glanced at me and laughed, a deep, throaty sound that washed over me.

'A million miles away.' I turned my face up to the sky to watch an eagle circling high in the air. 'You can't even believe when you're out here in the bush that the lodge is so nearby, with all its luxuries and posh guests.'

'My mum and dad bought this place thirty years ago. Kilingi means protector in Swahili, and that was their vision for the reserve. They wanted it to be a sanctuary for all the animals here. We're an approved release site for orphaned or injured animals, so we often have new arrivals here, and we offer guests some of the most spectacular big game sightings.' He paused. 'Do you know what I love about it here? The simplicity of it all. It's raw, it's primal, it's exhilarating. It's about survival on the very basic level. Whether you're watching the annual migration of zebra and wildebeest, or seeing a lion stalk its prey, or watching a jackal irritate a lizard, you never know what the next day will bring.' He swept a hand round in the air. 'People pay a lot of money to come out here and see all this. Do you know how many people would love to be doing what you're doing right now? Instead of sitting in their office, in their busy cities, worrying about what they look like or reading celebrity magazines to see whether Britney Spears has had a bum implant or not.'

I laughed. 'Has she?'

He shrugged. 'Who cares? It's not important in the scheme of things. Boob jobs, face lifts, tummy tucks, extreme diet crazes. People are so obsessed with things that don't matter. They're never happy with what they've got. They always want something else and something else, until greed takes over.'

Asha trotted up and shook her soaking wet body all over me.

'Yuck!' I pushed her off, but she rested her wet paws on my legs and then flopped her head on top of them, looking up at me as if to say, *Why aren't you playing with me?*

He glanced at me. 'I mean, what's wrong with the world?'

I mulled over what he said, feeling like he was judging me somehow. Before the accident, I was one of those girls who was obsessed with how I looked. Isn't that what every fifteen-year-old does? My friends and I would regularly pore over the celebrity magazines, trying to copy the stars' makeup and hair, trying to make ourselves look glamorous before we went into town. Giggling as the boys from school tried to chat to us. Spending hours in the shops choosing the latest eyeliner or lipstick. Not that it would make much difference to me now. No matter how much makeup I put on, or how fancy my hair was, it wasn't going to change how I looked, and I was one of those people he was talking about who wasn't happy with what I had.

A familiar bubbling anger rose to the surface. 'What do you know about it?' I said, the angry tone of my voice echoing in the stillness. 'When *you* look so perfect,' I blurted out, cringing inside at how that sounded. Now he'd think I fancied him or something. And how pathetic would that be? If we didn't have to spend so much time with each other because of Asha, there's no way he'd be seen dead near me.

He chuckled softly. 'No one's perfect.'

But that just made me angrier. 'Yeah, and isn't it always beautiful people who say things like that? "It's what's on the inside that counts."' I mimicked a sarcastic voice. 'You don't know anything about me.'

He lay back on one elbow, oblivious to my outburst, staring at the water. 'So tell me.'

'Tell you what?' I cried. 'What's it's like to be a freak?!' What it's like for everyone to laugh at you? What it's like to know that you can never get the job you want because who would want to employ someone like me? What it's like to be the object of ridicule?'

'That's what I'm trying to tell you. Out here, none of that matters. It's not like the animals care whether you've got eyelash extensions or a club foot.' He glanced at me. 'There are more serious things to worry about, like how long it will be before the last rhino gets wiped out, or whether there's a drought that's going to kill off some of our animals, or whether a whole herd of elephants has been murdered for its ivory.'

I leaped to my feet and marched back in the direction we'd come with Asha trundling behind, not caring if he was following or not as I simmered under the surface all the way home. No one as gorgeous as him could understand what it was like to be me.

As I arrived at our quarters, I heard him get into the Land Rover, but before he shut the door, he called out. 'I'll see you tomorrow morning.'

I whipped my head round, my eyes flashing with anger, and I could've sworn I saw the ghost of an amused smile on his face.

Chapter 9

'Can you pass me another fence post?' Zach said.

It was mid-morning and we were building the enclosure that Asha would eventually move into in front of our quarters. Zach thought the spot was perfect. There was enough shade for her, some trees that she'd be able to practice climbing on, and plenty of thick bushes. She was already three months old and the time had flown by. Her blue eyes had changed to a bright amber, and her coat had turned a deep golden colour with dark rosettes. Her paws seemed to have had a growth spurt ahead of her body, and they were huge. I'd managed to teach her early on to keep her claws sheathed when she was playing with me, otherwise I'd have been scratched to pieces.

Her latest craze was tugging the sheets off my bed with her teeth and dragging them underneath her body between her front paws to the door. Zach said it would help her learn how to drag prey up into the trees when she was older and gave me a tarpaulin sheet for her to use in the hope that she'd leave my bed alone. She sat under the shade of a nearby tree, watching us work with interest, her ears twitching.

I picked up a heavy panel and post that Zach had collected from Nairobi a few weeks before. The panels were made of thin iron bars so that Asha could see out into the bush beyond.

Expertly, Zach sank it in the ground and attached it to the one before it, examining his work carefully and thoughtfully as he went.

'I hate the thought of her having to be in here without me. Can't she just carry on staying in the house?' I asked.

He squinted up at me through the sunlight. 'We've been

over this before. She's not a pet. At this age her mum would be going off to hunt and leaving her on her own for long periods anyway. She needs to learn to be apart from you some of the time.'

I sighed and nodded. 'Do you want a drink?'

'I thought you'd never ask.'

I went into the cool of the house and Asha followed me in, thinking it was feeding time.

'Not yet, Asha.' I patted her on the top of her head as she looked up expectantly. She showed her disapproval by sitting on my foot and refusing to move. She was the size of a big dog by then and not exactly light.

I laughed at her mournful face, which she didn't like, so she moved into the corner of the room and sulked at me until I'd poured the drinks into glasses. By the time I headed outside she was back on my heels again, bounding out the door like all was forgiven.

We worked together until late afternoon when Asha trotted up to me, raring to go for her daily walk. She nudged her head into the back of my legs, making me lose my balance and collapse to the floor. This excited her even more and she jumped on top of me. I rolled around with her, playing and giggling as my hat fell off onto the ground. I picked up a piece of rope with a shoe tied to the end of it and ran round the new enclosure as she chased after it with boundless enthusiasm. Then I swung it high in the air and watched her gracefully leaping up to grab it in her mouth before I finally let her have her prize.

'Do I have to do all the work around here?' Zach smiled at us.

'Hey! I've been helping.' I smiled back, forgetting that my face was no longer hidden underneath the shadowed safety of my hat.

'We might as well walk now. She won't let us have any peace until we do.' I pushed Asha away, stood up, and dusted my shorts off.

Zach dropped a pair of pliers in his toolbox, and I fetched

Asha's lead.

'Come on, girl,' I said, but she needed no encouragement. She was off, tugging on the lead, only stopping to paw at a beetle or bat a twig, or to scratch her claws on some bark.

'I think she needs a climbing lesson. Leopards need to be as at home in the trees as they are on the ground. She'll have to drag her kill up there to feed if she wants to keep it away from scavenging hyenas or lions,' Zach said as we approached a small tree. 'This is a perfect nursery tree for her.'

I expertly climbed up the trunk and sat on a low hanging branch, my legs dangling either side.

Zach's jaw dropped open after watching my skilful ascent.

'What? Didn't you think girls from England could climb trees? Is it only people living in the African bush who climb that quick?' I mocked.

'Well, out here you've always got to be aware of the nearest tree. You never know when you might have to climb it in an instant to get out of the way of an animal. Where did you learn to climb so well?'

I shrugged. 'I've been climbing ever since I was five. I was always climbing the trees in our garden back home. If mum and dad couldn't find me in the house it was probably a given they'd find me in a tree somewhere, so Mum took me for lessons at our leisure centre climbing wall and that was it. I fell in love with it. It was like I could completely switch off from anything and just focus on getting to the top. I stopped going after the accident, but it must be like riding a bike. You never forget.'

Asha stood on her hind legs, front paws scratching at the base of the trunk, trying to reach me as Zach knelt on one knee, camera pressed to his face, filming us.

Instinctively, I touched the top of my head to push the brim of my hat down lower over my face and realised that it had fallen off. My gaze frantically swept the ground below, searching for it. Before I had time to panic about how disgusting I was going to look on film, Zach distracted me by laughing at Asha as she tried repeatedly to jump up the bark but kept falling off at the crucial moment, tumbling over and over until she got to her feet again with a determined look on her face.

I climbed back down and lifted her up the trunk, setting her paws onto the bark and holding her, waiting for her to get a grip. With a fearless and inquisitive nature, I didn't think it would be long before she got the hang of it, and I was rewarded for my faith in her a couple of hours later when she'd managed to stay in the tree for a whole ten minutes, even jumping back down and getting herself all the way up again without my help, using her claws for traction she could balance on even the thinnest branches.

'She's a natural,' I called down to Zach.

He slid the camera way from his face and turned it off. 'She's got a good teacher.' He slung the camera strap over one shoulder and his rifle over the other and climbed up, positioning himself on the branch next to Asha.

A commotion behind us drew my attention away from her, and Zach turned around to see what was happening.

A herd of impala were jumping around and snorting an alarm to each other.

'There's a lion,' Zach whispered, pointing out a large lioness, creeping up towards the herd, belly low in the dry grass. 'The impala leap around to confuse the lions. They can jump up to three metres high.'

I could feel the tension in the air as the herd began leaping and running in all directions. The lion sprinted forward with a burst of raw power. In all the mayhem, a smaller impala was separated from the others and ran around haphazardly, confused about what direction to go in.

Within seconds the lion was on top of it, holding it on the ground with a bite to the underside of its neck. The impala's legs twitched in the air as the lion held on tight.

My hands flew to my eyes and I squeezed them shut, not wanting to see the poor animal being torn apart. 'That's horrible.'

'It's part of the natural balance of our ecosystem, Jazz.'

I dropped my hands and turned around, looking at Asha as she tried to clamber down the tree and investigate what was going on in the distance. I grabbed onto her collar to keep her safely in the tree.

'Asha's going to be part of that ecosystem,' he said. 'And you will have to teach her to hunt. In two years time you'll *want* her to be killing as efficiently as that if there's any chance of her having a successful life out here. It's either that, or she'll be killed by a lion or other animal or starve to death.'

The thought of Asha killing another animal like that made me feel sick. An uneasy feeling settled in the pit of my stomach. Could I do this? Could I really teach this little leopard everything she needed to know when I couldn't even stand to see a lion kill its prey? What had I been thinking?

But when I looked down at Asha, a thought settled into my brain. This wasn't about me anymore. This was about saving an orphaned leopard from death in the wild and a sad lifetime locked in a zoo. It was about giving back what the poachers had taken away when they'd killed her mum – a right to her freedom. Life out here for animals was tough, and nature had her own laws. I had to do whatever it took to ensure her survival. Isn't that what mothers do? I thought about my own mum. How I'd caused the accident that led to her death. I couldn't be responsible for the same thing happening again.

I took a determined breath. 'You're right.'

'I'm always right.' The corner of his lip curled into a grin.

'Well, I wouldn't go that far.' I raised an eyebrow at him.

He pointed to a herd of elephants that had ambled up near the tree, keeping a wary eye on the lion. Even though an adult elephant was no match for a lion, a small calf could be.

'Look, this is one of our biggest elephant herds.' He pointed at a huge one out in front. 'That's Big Mama, the matriarch. The females live in one group in a little girly gang, and the males live in small bachelor groups.'

I knew all about gangs of girls. The ones at school, who were supposed to have been my friends and made my life a misery. The things they wrote about me on the toilet walls and the things they said. But this beautiful herd of twenty-five elephants was nothing like them. They ranged from Big Mama, who was huge, to small calves wandering close to their mothers. For such large animals, I was surprised at how graceful and peaceful they seemed while they slowly fed on the acacia trees and bushes.

'You see that one in the middle? We call her Houdini,' he said. 'She witnessed her mother and the rest of her herd being shot by hunters at a game farm in South Africa. Big rich guys think it's great fun to fly in for a quick shooting trip and pay a fortune to kill the animals, then fly out again with a trophy or two. They have so much money they think they can do exactly what they want. For two days Houdini stood by her mother's body, trying to suckle, until the farm owners managed to get her away from the area. They were keeping her until she was old enough to grow tusks so she'd be more attractive to the hunters, but she was so stressed by what she'd seen that she kept charging through the electric fencing they had. After the third time it happened she was captured by the nearest National Park and relocated here to stop her stampeding the local village. Dad and I slowly introduced her to our herd and she's never tried to escape since she arrived.' He took a satisfied breath. 'Elephants have such sophisticated emotions and are so sensitive, they can see and feel things that we don't even know about. Like us, they feel grief and often touch the bones or the bodies of their dead and show sadness. They also cry tears when they're traumatised or held captive. Imagine how she must've felt when she saw all that.' He gazed at her. 'Whenever it seems like things are getting on top of me, I just come out here and look at them. Watch this.' He climbed down from the tree, keeping an eye on the lioness that was busy feeding. With his hands round his mouth, he called out Houdini's name.

Houdini stopped grazing on a bush and stood stock still, her mouth open and her trunk lifting up, as if sniffing the air.

As Big Mama had her fill and ambled away, Houdini turned around and walked slowly towards us, her trunk swinging.

'Come here, girl,' he said softly to her.

Houdini's ears spread, picking up his voice.

I gasped at this huge animal coming towards Zach, trunk outstretched, wondering what she would do.

'How are you doing, girl?' Zach looked up at her.

She stopped in front of him and blinked her long eyelashes. Then she reached up her trunk and touched his head with the tip, moving it around his shoulders, letting him pat her.

I watched, eyes wide with amazement at this huge wild animal actively seeking out Zach and saying hello.

After a few minutes she dropped her trunk, turned slowly, and moseyed away.

'There's nothing like a bit of elephant love.' Zach looked up and grinned. 'They can detect one scent particle amongst a million. They can tell which animals live where on the reserve, which have recently been killed, where to get much needed salt when the droughts come, and when the rains will fall. They know which rangers are out here today and can pick up sounds for miles around. Elephants use infrasound, which are low rumbles that travel a long way. It's so low humans can't actually hear it.' He paused with a sad expression. 'It just makes me sick to think that anyone would want to slaughter such a complex and sensitive creature for their two front teeth.' He stood and gazed at Houdini's retreating form as she rejoined her herd. 'You see, this is what I mean by showing you. Until you witness the things that animals do, you'll never begin to understand the depth of their intelligence and feelings.'

Houdini greeted Big Mama with a touching of trunks and I felt the emotion and passion in Zach's voice. It made me sick, too. Watching them made me wonder how they could be killed when we were supposed to be living in a civilised world. Is that what people called progress?

'Isn't hunting wild game banned?' I asked.

'Hunting is still legal in some parts of Africa, even though there are restrictions in place for dealing in rhino horn or ivory. In the eighties there were hardly any rhino or elephants left here because of their slaughter, and the numbers of antelope and big cats had dwindled to desperate levels. Leopards were all but wiped out due to the fur trade. The bans in horn and ivory helped to increase numbers initially, but we're getting back to where we were again with an increase in demand. It's all very well having controls in place, but they're easy to evade and not effective in protecting these animals.' He shook his head sadly and took a deep breath, tearing his eyes away from the herd. 'Come on, we'll be late for the party.'

'What party?' I said, climbing down and reattaching Asha's lead.

'I told you weeks ago. The head of the Kenyan Wildlife Service is coming to discuss some new initiatives to try and eliminate poaching. Mum and Dad are hosting a party for him.'

'I'm not coming,' I said.

He stopped abruptly, turning around, and I nearly bumped into him.

I quickly took a step back, desperately trying to ignore the fact that our faces were inches apart. I looked down at the ground, blushing, and felt his hot breath on my cheeks.

'But he'll want to meet you,' he said. 'He knows what we're doing with Asha, and it will be great publicity to try and get the anti-poaching message out there.'

I could feel his eyes boring into me as I stared at a line of ants on the ground.

'Please. Do it for me,' he whispered. 'We've invited our friends from the Mumbi Game Reserve, too. It will be a good chance for you to get to know more people.'

But I didn't want to get to know more people. I was happy

the way things were. In the weeks that I'd spent time with Zach, we'd settled into an easy friendship. A friendship I hadn't had since the accident. I looked forward more and more to our walks together and the time we spent doing things with Asha. But I wasn't ready to meet and be stared at or gossiped about by a whole load of strangers. Dad and I ate our meals at home, and I hardly ever went to the lodge since that first day at work. I wasn't doing it for a party, either. No. I just wasn't ready.

'I can't do it.' I carried on walking. 'You know as much about Asha as me. You'll be fine on your own. You don't need me.'

'Your dad will be there.'

'I don't care. I'm not going.'

'You can be so stubborn.'

'And you can be bossy and a know-it-all.'

'Who, me?' he asked with mock horror. 'You must be talking about someone else.'

I chuckled and it lifted the mood as we walked back to our quarters in silence.

'If you change your mind, it starts at eight,' he said, jumping into the Land Rover and driving towards the lodge.

Fat chance of that.

I glanced down at Asha, who plonked herself next to my feet, staring up expectantly for some milk. 'Come on, girl, let's get you fed.'

I gave Asha her milk in a bowl now, which I mixed with minced meat, then turned my attention to cooking something for me. Since I didn't eat at the lodge, Chef and Jenna sent Dad down to the house with food, and I was learning how to cook from Chef's recipes. Apart from Asha and Zach, it was the only other interest in my life, and I found that I loved creating new dishes, waiting excitedly as I watched Dad take his first bite to see if he was enjoying it. I must've been doing something right because I began to put weight on and my bony frame was filling out into slender curves.

After making a chicken curry, I took myself off to the

hammock on the veranda to watch the sunset while Dad got ready for the party. Asha was getting too big to jump in there with me, but it didn't stop her trying. In the end, she settled for squashing me as she launched herself onto the hammock sideways, paws dangling off the edges while we swung from side to side. I stroked her head and she licked me with her rough, sandpaper tongue until it tickled, then snuggled against my legs and rested her chin in my hand as I giggled at her.

'How do I look?' Dad came out of the house decked out in smart black trousers, a white shirt, and a deep purple tie. The last time I'd seen him look so posh was when he'd taken Mum out for their anniversary dinner a few weeks before the accident.

The tears prickled in my eyes.

I wish you were here, Mum.

'You look really nice,' I croaked.

He frowned slightly. 'If you're not up to going, I understand, but it would be really nice if you did.'

I shook my head, trying to blink away the tears.

Oh, Mum, I miss you so much.

He leaned over and kissed my forehead before giving Asha a quick pat on the head. 'I'll see you later, then. If you change your mind, you know where we are.'

'Have a good time,' I mumbled.

After he'd gone I carried on watching the sunset and talking to Mum in my head, telling her about my day, which was something I'd started doing ever since I'd found Asha. Wherever she was now, I was sure she could hear me.

When the sky turned black I reached down for the cookbook that Chef had lent me and flicked through it, looking for something to try the following night.

The loud rumbling of a Land Rover a few minutes later broke into my culinary thoughts.

'Did you forget something?' I shouted to Dad as I heard the vehicle door open and shut.

But it was Zach's voice that drifted up the steps towards

me. 'I just wanted to see if you'd changed your mind.'

He took the stairs two at a time, and when I saw him, an involuntary gasp escaped from my lips. His dark hair was neatly cropped and his smooth, square jaw line almost shone in the lights. He wore black trousers that skimmed every inch of his well-toned legs, and a light blue shirt that seemed to bring out the unusual colour of his eyes. Eyes that were watching me intently as my mouth hung open. He looked amazing.

'You look...' What could I say? I didn't want to tell him he looked gorgeous. 'Er...nice,' I settled for, turning my attention to stroking Asha so I wouldn't have to look at him anymore.

'Thanks.' He walked over and sat on the chair next to me.

'You've had your hair cut,' I said.

'I did it with clippers. Not very often you get a top hairdresser around here.' I heard the smile in his voice. 'Do you fancy coming?'

I shook my head. How could I ever compete with all the people that would be there, decked out in their nice clothes, hair perfectly done, makeup glittering on their flawless faces?

He was silent for a while, and I willed him to go away.

'You can't measure self worth by how you look,' he said softly. 'It's what you do that counts.'

'And I suppose you're going to give me another lecture about how beauty is on the inside,' I snapped.

He stood up to leave. 'No.' He looked down at me for a few moments as I picked up the cookbook and pretended to read. My eyes scanning what now looked like gobbledygook on the page. 'You have to face your fears, Jazz, or else you'll drown in them.'

I sighed, hoping to get the message through that the conversation was over, but he wasn't finished.

'Everyone has scars. Whether they're on the outside or inside, everyone's got them. They're just a reminder that we've survived something big and come out stronger.' His words drifted into my head and he stood there until the silence became too loud, and he slowly walked back to the Land Rover.

As I heard him disappearing into the night, I dropped the book on the floor with a loud slap and stared at the moon coming over the horizon, thinking about what he'd said for a long time.

Maybe he was right. Maybe I should go out and start meeting people. I knew it wasn't healthy to be a recluse for the rest of my life. After everything Zach had done for me, maybe I should show my appreciation of our friendship by going.

'What should I do, Mum?' I whispered.

I waited to see if she'd send me some kind of sign but nothing happened.

Asha looked at me expectantly, the fur on her forehead crinkling up. 'What would you do?' I asked Asha, but she just licked her paw. Not very helpful.

I pushed her gently off me and walked to my bedroom. What on earth could I possibly wear? Before we'd arrived, Dad had made me buy loads of clothes, but instead of going to the shops for them, where I'd be stared at by bitchy sales girls, I'd ordered them online. I had plenty of practical clothes like shorts and jeans and T-shirts for being out in the bush, but I didn't have a party dress. It wasn't like I ever thought I'd ever need one again.

I rummaged around in my cupboard, pulling potential things out and throwing them onto the bed. Asha thought it was great fun to grab hold of an item in her mouth and run around the room with it before diving under the bed to slobber on it.

'Get off!' I tugged at a yellow sun dress with white flowers and heard a ripping sound. 'Asha, no!'

She'd come to understand the word 'no' and dropped it, looking sheepish. I picked up the now slobbery, ripped dress and sighed, throwing it onto the floor. Asha looked between me and the dress, as if saying, *Can I have it now? Go on, please.*

I sighed, fearing that maybe it was a sign from Mum that I shouldn't go. Plonking myself down on the edge of the bed, I stared into the wardrobe until I spotted a red cotton sundress with thin straps that tied at the shoulder and fell just above my knees. Yanking it off the hanger, I pulled it on and smoothed it down. Next, I brushed my hair with a shaky hand until it felt smooth and silky, then shook my head so the sides fell over my face as much as possible. This was a good as it was ever going to get.

I picked up Asha's rubber ball and threw it out into the hallway for her. Like lightning, she dashed out of the room and pounced on it, her needle-sharp milk teeth sinking into it.

'I won't be long,' I told her, then wagged a finger at her as I said, 'Don't chew on anything, and don't scratch at the furniture again.'

She gave me a quick look before turning her attention back to the ball, and I grabbed a torch from the sideboard by the front door and slipped outside, shutting it quietly behind me.

My hands still shook as I turned on the torch and walked towards the lodge with the sounds of tinkling laughter mixed with soft music and conversation drifting towards me.

I reached the empty reception building and wiped my sweaty palms down my dress, taking a deep breath.

You can do this. You can do this.

I followed the sounds towards the dining room and hovered in the entrance, watching the scene in front of me as a knot formed in my stomach.

Richard, Jenna, and Dad were in a deep animated conversation with a distinguished-looking black man. Other guests milled around with drinks in their hands or picking at a sumptuous buffet laid out in the centre of the room. People mingled with each other, laughing and smiling. They all had one thing in common. None of them looked like me.

My gaze searched the room for Zach until it finally rested on him. He stood in the corner of the room with a beautiful brunette who was probably the same age as him. She had a figure-hugging, short black dress on and strappy high heels. Her hair hung in ringlets around her heart-shaped face, and she was perfectly made up. She whispered something into his ear and his arm slid around her waist, pulling her closer as he threw his head back and laughed.

My heart raced, and I felt fingers of anger and jealousy twist my insides.

What had I been thinking? I was never going to be able to compete with these people. I was never going to have a boyfriend. I was never going to get married and have kids. I was never going to find someone who loved me like Dad loved Mum. I would always be on the outside looking in.

I backed away from the doorway and stumbled blindly all the way home as hot tears streaked down my face.

Chapter 10

One morning, Asha was stalking a beetle in the bush. She stood frozen, her belly low to the ground, eyeing it with a focused determination.

'I'll miss our walk this afternoon,' Zach said while I watched her. 'I'm going over to Mumbi Game Reserve to see Kira and I won't be back until late.'

I looked up sharply.

Kira. I bet she was the girl from the party. The thought of him with her made me feel sick and I didn't know why. It wasn't as if we were anything other than friends, and it wasn't like you could expect someone as gorgeous as him not to have a girlfriend.

Asha pounced on the beetle with her front paws and it disappeared into her mouth. She rolled it around for a while before deciding it didn't taste very nice and spat it out with a disgusted look.

'She's–' Zach started, but I cut him off.

'Well, have a good time,' I said, my voice coming out harsher than I intended. I didn't want to hear about how fantastic Kira was.

He raised confused eyebrows at my tone of voice and said, 'Don't go off into the bush on your own.' He gave me a warning look. 'OK?'

'Yes, *Dad.*' I gave him a salute.

He grinned as we arrived back at Asha's enclosure, and I stood there staring at his retreating back until he disappeared, seeing the picture of him and Kira looking so cosy together at the party in my head.

By the time Asha's afternoon walk was due, she was restless and full of energy, so I tried to distract her by getting her food ready. She was only on two meals of milk a day now, and I'd introduced her to solid meat. I fed her in the enclosure so she'd get used to it and it wouldn't be so hard for her when the time came to leave her in there overnight on her own. Zach had told me that leopards had a very varied diet: antelope, gazelle, warthogs, impala, zebra, rodents, and even fish, birds, lizards, hares, and other small prey. Today she was having hare. Yum. She still had her milk teeth, so she wasn't able to rip open the animal herself, which meant Zach had to cut it open for her.

I hadn't managed to get over my squeamishness about handling the carcasses. It was one of the worst jobs of being a leopard mum. I pulled on some rubber gloves and turned my head away as I picked it up by a leg and set it down on the ground in her enclosure.

Licking her lips in anticipation, she bounded over to it, tugging at the flesh and spitting out the fur with a frown. I sat next to her on the ground, staring off into the distance. Why should Asha miss out on her walk just because Zach was off seeing his girlfriend? The lions here were pretty used to seeing people out and about on safari, and most of the time they'd ignore you. If they did approach too close, I'd seen Zach frighten them off by shouting and waving his arms, and I was perfectly capable of doing the same. What was the worst that could happen?

After Asha finished licking the bones clean, I stood up and called to her. She followed eagerly as we walked off into the bush but kept stopping and looking around for Zach.

'He's not coming,' I said. 'He's got better things to do than hang around with us.' And that's when the realisation struck me.

I missed him.

A loud grumble emanating from deep within Asha's throat interrupted my thoughts. She stood stock still, one paw still raised in mid-walk. I looked down sharply at her strange behaviour and saw she was staring at a group of about six lionesses crouched behind some bushes a short distance away and well-hidden. If it hadn't been for Asha, I wouldn't even have noticed them. They were carefully watching a herd of wildebeest, sizing them up as a potential meal.

I grabbed tightly on Asha's lead, winding it around my hand until it dug in, and watched two of the lionesses move silently to the side of the unsuspecting herd. Two others flanked the opposite side. Another lioness brought up the rear. When one of the wildebeest looked up, the lions remained like statues, their golden coats blending into the dry grasses. I could feel an electric tension in the air as the lionesses silently communicated their teamwork to each other.

In a burst of speed, the lionesses bolted towards the herd. In their rush to get away, the wildebeest honked and kicked up the dusty ground, but in the panic, one of the adolescents ran straight for one of the lionesses. In seconds it was on the ground, with one lioness strangling it in a choke hold, and the others already biting into its rump.

I turned my face away, not wanting to see the carnage, and then I felt Asha tugging on the lead. I looked down at her as she struggled to get away from me. Then I saw two of the lionesses running towards us, their muzzles bright red with blood.

There was no time to think, I just ran, dragging Asha behind me. There was a nearby tree. If we could make it up there, we'd be safe.

I reached the tree and started climbing, my skills instantly kicking in.

'Come on, Asha.' I pulled the lead, the urgency in my voice and her natural instincts spurring her to jump expertly onto the trunk behind me. All the climbing lessons I'd given her had paid off, and she moved upward through the branches with a natural ease.

We reached a fork in the trunk about four metres up, and I looked down at two of the lionesses pacing round the bottom of the tree, their eyes fixed on us with unflinching coldness. They roared a sickening death rumble, the black tips of their tails lashing around with fury.

Still we climbed higher, the blood pounding in my ears and my breath coming in panicked pants. Asha misjudged one of the branches and her back legs slipped.

I gasped and grabbed her collar.

She clung onto the branch and quickly found her balance again, her back paws seeking out a new section of branch.

The lions jumped up the trunk. The bigger one fell back down, but the other one kept coming, climbing up the big lower branches with ease until it reached the fork. I didn't have a clue lions could climb, and I just hoped that we could do it better.

The lioness in the tree tentatively tested the upper branches with a paw before climbing higher, while the lioness on the ground paced around, looking up at us, eyes flashing in the dusk. I could hear the rest of the pride snarling and snapping at each other as they devoured the wildebeest.

I held my breath and crept higher, making sure Asha was close behind. She was panting, her eyes wide and her pupils huge. There was no way we could go any further. The branches at the top were too thin and wouldn't be able to hold our weight. I sat with my legs either side of a branch, my thighs squeezed together, firmly fixing me in place as I held onto Asha's collar tightly. She lay next to me, balanced on a branch, her tail flicking nervously in the air as she stared down at the lionesses.

I watched the lioness in the tree stop on one of the branches, looking up at us. She bared her teeth and roared at us, trying to work out how to go higher.

The lioness on the ground jumped onto the trunk and began to climb, too.

I swallowed hard.

The lioness up the tree climbed awkwardly onto another branch and it snapped under her weight, sending her crashing to the ground. The other lioness jumped down and landed next to her, nudging at her face.

By the wildebeest carcass, I heard the roar of a male lion

and the two lionesses' ears flicked back. They gave us one last look up in the tree before rushing off back to their kill.

I exhaled a breath and realised I was shaking. Asha silently watched them retreat with an intense stare, and I buried my face in her fur.

As the dark night surrounded us, I could hear them feasting and knew it wouldn't be safe to get down until they'd gone. We'd just have to wait it out.

I stroked Asha as my heartbeat slowed down and my breathing returned to normal. After what felt like at least an hour had passed, I had pins and needles in my legs and my head was aching with a post-adrenaline rush. I didn't particularly relish the idea of spending the night out here. There could be hyenas attracted by the lion's kill, or even other leopards roaming around. And they could definitely climb trees like a pro.

When the lionesses and the large male had gorged themselves, they lay on the ground, their bellies swollen, lying like sentries to guard what was left of the bone and flesh. Under the glint of the full moon rising I saw a hyena scout looking on before rushing off to fetch the scavenger party.

Asha had grown bored of watching the scene below and settled her head on her front paws, snoozing. I wished I had the same ability to switch off. It looked pretty likely that we might have to spend the night here.

More throaty roaring got my attention again as a group of hyenas circled the lions, snapping at them. The male lion lazily turned around and bared his teeth in a snarl at them but refused to move. A couple of the lionesses chased the hyenas away, but as soon as their backs were turned to walk off and rejoin the pride, the hyenas came back. After about three quarters of an hour of this, the lions seemed to get irritated with them, and with a throaty rasping cry, they slunk off into the night, deciding the carcass wasn't worth the hassle and leaving the hyenas cackling away, crunching on the last of the bones.

I rubbed at my neck, which was aching with stiffness, and heard the distant sound of a Land Rover. It was probably Dad sending out a hunting party for me.

I saw the spotlights bouncing over the ground in the distance and shouted, 'Over here!' But I didn't know if they'd be able to hear me.

The lights must've caught the hyenas feeding and settled on them as it came closer.

'Over here!' I cried repeatedly, not wanting to try and stand up to wave in case I fell out.

As the Land Rover reached the hyenas, they scattered, and I heard Zach's voice yell, 'What the hell do you think you're doing?'

The Land Rover stopped beneath the tree and I scrambled down with Asha close behind and we sprinted towards the vehicle. I opened the door and picked Asha up, pushing her inside and jumping in, nearly sitting on top of her in the process.

He glared at me through hooded eyes. 'What on earth were you thinking?' he yelled.

It was the first time I'd ever seen him lose his temper, and it caught me off guard.

My mouth dropped open in shock and refused to work.

'You could've been killed!' he shouted, eyes bright with anger. He thrust the gear stick into first with enough force to pull it off and drove forward. 'Don't *ever* do that to me again,' he barked.

Chapter 11

The next day I waited nervously for Zach to arrive for our early morning walk. He hadn't spoken to me all the way home, and I didn't know if he was even going to turn up.

I sat on the wooden steps of the veranda, arms locked around my knees, head resting on top of them. Asha was playing in her enclosure with the door open, launching herself at the old tyre I'd tied to the lower branches in one of the trees and hanging off it as she swung through the air. It would've been funny if I wasn't in such a bad mood.

I'd done a stupid thing. It was all very well risking my own life, but what about Asha? I was supposed to be protecting her, and my stubbornness could've cost us our lives. I felt so stupid and disgusted with myself.

Dad hurried down the steps. 'Have a good day, I'll see you later.' He stopped at the Land Rover and looked back at me. 'Don't worry, you two will make it up. I could've killed you myself last night, I was that worried about you. You had everyone out looking for you.' He frowned.

'I'm sorry,' I apologised to him for what must've been the hundredth time since I arrived home last night. He'd been so angry I thought his head was going to explode.

'Well, maybe you'll realise now why we keep telling you not to go out into the bush on your own.' He frowned.

I nodded glumly.

His face softened and he blew me a kiss and drove off, leaving me mentally kicking myself.

Maybe Zach wouldn't even speak to me again. He'd been so annoyed with me I could practically see the steam coming out of his ears. He hadn't even said goodbye when he'd dropped me off. How could I jeopardise a friendship that had become so special to me?

I went inside to get a glass of water and heard a Land Rover pull up. Rushing to the window, I saw Zach get out and then lean back inside, reaching for something.

I set the glass back on the kitchen worktop, my heart racing, and rushed outside. By the time I'd got down the steps, he was walking towards me with a rifle slung over his shoulder on a strap and a box of ammunition in his hands.

'I know I'm a pain in the arse but there's no need to shoot me,' I joked, trying to lighten the mood.

He didn't laugh.

I searched his face, looking for signs that his anger had dissipated. It wasn't looking good.

I glanced down at the floor, kicking the dirt with the toe of my boot. 'I'm sorry about last night.'

'It's not a game out here, Jazz.'

'I know, and I'm sorry.'

'Well, if you're not going to listen and go off and do stupid things on your own, then I think you'd better learn how to shoot.'

I glanced up, meeting his admonishing gaze. 'I'm not going to shoot an animal.'

'You don't have to shoot an animal. But you can fire a warning shot if you get cornered and most of the animals will run away.'

I looked at the gun. Maybe it would be a good idea to learn some kind of protection. And at least it meant he'd still have to talk to me.

'Shut Asha in her enclosure and we'll go,' he said.

I stared at him. 'Can't she come too? She's never been shut in there without me.'

'No. The way you go about things you'll probably end up shooting her. Plus, if she hears the shot, she'll probably bolt. In the wild her mum would be busy hunting and leaving her to her own devices, so you've got to get her used to being without you some of the time.'

I glanced at Asha playing in the tree.

'In a few weeks time she'll have to sleep in the enclosure on her own. Let her get used to you being away gradually.' His tone softened.

I walked up to the enclosure, closed the door and locked the padlock, slipping the key into my pocket. Asha rushed up to the door and pushed against it with her head, making a whining noise. She looked up through the iron bars with an expression of sadness.

I slid my fingers through and stroked her nose and under her chin. 'Don't worry, Asha, I'll be back before you know it.'

And as Zach led me away from the enclosure and into the bush I kept glancing behind me, seeing Asha's forlorn face and feeling the guilt suffocating me.

'It's for her own good,' Zach said.

'I know.'

He draped an arm casually around my shoulder as we walked, and I felt my mood lifting. 'Don't worry about her. She'll be fine. I know what I'm talking about.'

After we'd walked to a deserted area near the edge of the reserve, he stopped and looked around.

'Here's a good place to learn. There aren't many animals around here at the moment.'

I breathed a sigh of relief. The last thing I wanted to do was accidentally shoot one.

There was a large tree to our right and a cluster of rocks straight ahead.

'I'm not sure about this.' I glanced at the rifle.

He swung the strap off his shoulder and held it out. 'It's for your own safety. You never know what will happen out here, and you always have to be prepared for the unexpected. Don't worry, it's not loaded. Yet.'

I took it. It felt heavy and cumbersome.

'It's heavier than I thought,' I said.

'That's a lighter one than the rangers carry. It doesn't have any kickback, either, so you shouldn't suffer from any pain in your shoulder when you use it.'

After giving me a lesson about the different parts of the gun and how to load the cartridges, he stood next to me and rested it against his shoulder. 'You need to get the most stable balance when aiming at a target. If your posture is off, your muscles will be taking the strain, and that can add wobble to the rifle.' He held it steadily, pointing in front of him. 'If you're aiming from a standing position, you'll need to find your centre of balance. Keep the balance of the rifle and your body vertical and directly over your feet. They should be planted at shoulder width apart to keep the gun steady, and you'll probably find that keeping the pressure on the balls of your feet will give you more balance and control.' He glanced at me to make sure I was listening. 'Keep the butt of the gun into your shoulder, and find a comfortable position for your trigger hand on the gun.' He glanced down at the rifle. 'Your hand should be resting underneath it in a position that's comfortable to hold its weight. Try a few arm hold positions and see what's comfortable and stable for you.' He held the gun out, lifted the butt up to my shoulder, and pointed it out into the distance. 'Now you try.'

I looked down at my feet and moved them to shoulder-width distance. 'That feels uncomfortable,' I said.

'Keep your legs straight but still relaxed. You don't want to force your knees into a locked position. If you move your hips forward slightly, it will help your left elbow rest against you.' He rested his hands on my hips and moved them forward a notch.

I raised the gun to my face again so he wouldn't see me blushing or read the signs on my face that would surely give away how much I enjoyed his closeness.

'How's that?' he asked.

'Better,' I managed to croak.

'Your shoulders are tense.'

'I've got a gun in my hands for the first time. Of course they're tense!'

He rested his hands on my shoulders and pressed them

down slightly, relaxing my muscles.

A tingling sensation travelled up my spine.

'Lean your upper body slightly to the rear foot. That's better.' His hands stayed on my shoulders.

Oh, yes, that's much better.

'Now look down the sight and get used to seeing through it,' he said.

I did as instructed and he removed his hands.

'Lift it up a bit higher.' He leaned his hard chest into my back and his arms came round me, resting on the outer side of my arms.

I leaned into him, feeling the heat from his body through his shirt. I could feel his breath on the back of my hair as he spoke and I felt goosebumps on my skin.

'That's right,' he said.

He dropped his arms and stepped back, but even though he was no longer pressed into me, I could still feel the warm afterglow of his touch.

'You see those rocks? I want you to aim for the centre of them.' He took the gun off me and loaded some cartridges.

I jumped when I heard them click into place.

He looked up at me and smiled reassuringly. 'You'll be fine. It just takes a bit of getting used to.'

'How old were you when you learned?'

'Dad taught me when I was about six.'

'You learned to shoot when you were six?' I asked, jaw dropping open.

He shrugged. 'It's a different world out here from what you're used to. What were you doing when you were six?'

'Probably having princess parties and playing with my Barbie. I bet you're going to tell me that you could repair a Land Rover with a piece of chewing gum and lasso a wildebeest at that age, too.' I raised my eyebrows.

He chuckled and took the radio from its holster on his hip. 'All units, I'll be firing shots for the next half an hour. Repeat, I'll be firing shots for the next half an hour.' He rattled off his coordinates and the rangers confirmed they'd received his radio call.

'We have to let each other know when any shots are fired, otherwise they'll think there are poachers in the area.' He handed me the gun, waiting until I was comfortable with my stance and rifle positioning.

'That's it. Look through the sight and aim in between the crosshairs at the rocks. Position it so the middle of the crosshairs is directly on what you want to shoot at.'

I inhaled a tense breath. Held it. I concentrated so hard on the crosshairs that my eyes started to water. I squeezed the trigger and saw a chunk of dry soil in front of the rocks fly up in the air as the gunshot echoed like a crash of thunder. A few birds scattered from their perches in the tree next to us.

I exhaled a loud breath and lowered the gun, frowning. 'I wasn't aiming for the ground.'

'Don't worry. Try again.'

I set up my stance and gun position and went through the same flow of movements. Inhale. Sight. Shoot. Exhale. This time I hit the base of the rocks.

'That's better. Keep going.'

I lifted the gun up again, trying hard to aim closer to the centre of the rocks. As I was just pulling the trigger, a flash of something black in the air shooting across my sightline distracted my attention and my arm jerked to the right unintentionally as the shot rang out.

'Ow!' Zach yelled, clutching the top of his backside and twisting around to look at it.

I dropped the gun on the floor as if it were on fire, my hands pressed to my cheeks. 'Oh, my God, what did I do?'

'I think you shot me.' He twisted around to look at a hole about four centimetres long that had sliced through the back of his shorts.

All the blood in my body seemed to pool at the bottom of my feet in shock. 'How could I shoot you? I wasn't even pointing that way?' I cried. 'I'm so sorry. Does it hurt?'

'Of course it hurts!' He unbuttoned the top of his shorts and pulled the waistband down slightly, revealing the top curve of his right buttock, twisting around frantically to get a good look. 'Damn. I can't see it properly. It's stinging like hell. I need to know if there's a bullet in there or if it's just grazed.' He turned his back to me. 'Have a look.'

Before I could even think about the fact that I was staring at his very well-toned behind, I took in the red, inch-long graze and the blood that trickled from it.

'Well?' he asked urgently. 'How bad is it?'

'Erm…it just looks like a graze to me.'

'You can't see a bullet in there?' he said, eyes wild.

I peered a little closer. 'Stop moving about, I can't see properly with you wriggling.'

'Is there a bullet in there, or not?' he snapped.

I pressed two fingers onto his warm flesh, pulling the skin at the top of the graze taut and looking into the wound.

Oh, my God, I'm touching his bum!

If it wasn't so serious, I'd probably have been dying of embarrassment.

'Nope, there's no bullet in there. It's about half a centimetre deep and about two centimetres long.'

He nodded towards the Land Rover. 'There's a first aid kit in the glove box. Can you clean the wound with antiseptic and stick a dressing over the top? Wounds can get infected pretty quick out here.'

I ran to the Land Rover in a flash and returned with the first aid kit. My hands were shaking so much that it took me a few goes to click open the catch. I found the antiseptic as Zach glanced from the rock to the tree on our right-hand side with an angry frown.

Ripping open a sterile packet of cotton wool, I poured some iodine onto it and wiped it against the wound.'

'Argh!' Zach cried.

'Sorry! Is it stinging?'

'Just do it.' He held his breath.

When I was sure I'd wiped it down sufficiently, I opened a sterile dressing and pressed it to his buttock, making sure it was stuck down well. 'There. It's all done.'

He pulled up his shorts and buttoned them. Then he limped slowly to the tree and pointed to a nick in the bark before looking back at me. 'Your shot flew off the rock and ricocheted against the tree. I'm guessing it was a bit of bark that shot off and sliced through me.

'I'm so sorry,' I repeated, beginning to sound like a stuck record.

He picked up the gun and slung the strap over his shoulder. 'Come on, we'd better get back. There's no point in doing any more today, I don't know which other part of me you're going to shoot.' He winced as he walked off.

I gulped and caught up with him. 'I feel really bad.'

'Not as bad as I feel. I was going to teach you to drive, too, but now I'm not so sure. You'll probably run over me, or something.'

We looked at each other and then both burst out laughing as the serious side of the situation wore off and the funny side registered with relief.

It felt good to laugh. So good.

'I can't believe you shot me in the arse!' He chuckled.

'It's just a graze, you wimp!' I laughed harder.

'We'd probably better keep this between ourselves. Your Dad would be worried sick if he thought you'd shot someone.'

I mimed zipping up my lips and throwing away the key, trying not to laugh. When we arrived back at our quarters, Dad was sitting on the veranda with a sandwich and a glass of ice tea. 'Hi, guys. How's your day going?'

I looked at Zach conspiratorially, and his eyes danced with amusement.

Dad motioned for us to sit down. 'Are you all right, Zach? You're limping.'

'Yes, I've just pulled a muscle.' He smiled reassuringly at Dad.

Dad nodded. 'Well, have a seat and I'll get you a cold drink. You both look really hot.'

'Er...no, thanks, I prefer to stand.' Zach looked at me.

The corners of my lips curled up into an unstoppable smile, and we burst out laughing again.

Chapter 12

Asha was limping by the time Zach and I got back from our walk one evening. She made it home and plonked herself down in front of the steps, licking at her front paw.

I picked up her paw and looked, examining it closely as Zach peered over my shoulder. 'I can see a thorn stuck in her pad. It looks quite deep. I don't want to pull it out in case it snaps off.' Our quarters were in darkness, so I knew that Dad probably wasn't home, but I called out to him anyway.

No reply.

Zach unclipped the radio from his belt and called him. About five minutes later, he appeared in the Land Rover. Dad jumped out and grabbed his vet bag.

'How is she?' He looked down at Asha busy licking and trying to gnaw on the thorn with her teeth.

'She's OK, but it must be hurting her,' I said.

Dad bent down in front of her as I sat next to her and pulled her head away, resting it in my lap. He picked up her paw, studied it, then reached into his bag for a pair of long tweezers. Holding her paw tight, he expertly pulled the thorn straight out and held it up for us to see.

'All finished.' Dad smiled. 'Her pad might be a little tender for a while, but no harm done. These thorns are a hazard for the animals. If they get stuck in they can become infected.'

Asha pulled her head away from me and went back to licking her paw.

'Are you keeping her in the enclosure tonight?' Dad asked me.

I looked uncertainly between him and Zach. Although she now spent longer in there during the daytime, I'd been putting off leaving her in there at night. She was getting far too big to sleep on my bed, and often wanted to wrestle me in the middle of the night, but still, the thought of leaving her alone at night worried me.

'Well, if she's got a sore paw, maybe it's not such a good idea,' I said.

'She's almost six months old. You've got to do it sooner or later,' Zach said.

I gnawed on my bottom lip. 'What if her wound gets infected, or she misses me too much or–'

'She needs to get used to it. It's not like she would be sleeping on a bed in the wild,' Dad said. 'Plus, she snores.' He grinned.

'She does not!' I covered her ears so she couldn't ear them talking about her.

Zach agreed with Dad. 'She needs to start tonight.'

I looked at Asha, feeling my heart sink. I should've been glad that she'd made it this far, but the thought of us being separated broke my heart. I didn't even want to think about what would happen in the future when she was released back into the wild. How would I get through the day without her?

I felt the weight of their gazes on me. 'You're ganging up on me,' I moaned.

They looked at each other and shrugged.

'No one said this was going to be easy.' Dad gave me a sympathetic smile.

'Well, what if I sleep out here with her tonight? You know, just to get her used to being in the enclosure at night?'

Dad and Zach glanced at each other.

'At least that will break her in gently.' I raised hopeful eyebrows in their direction.

'You'll get bitten to death out here by mosquitoes.' Dad shook his head softly.

Zach thought about it for a while. 'I guess it couldn't hurt. For *one* night only, though.'

I leaped up, punching the air. 'Yes!'

'Your Dad's right, though. You're going to need a mossie

net to put over you or you'll be suffering tomorrow.' Zach stroked his chin. 'Look, if you really want to do this, I'll go and get some camping supplies from the lodge that we use for overnight walking safaris, and I'll bring back a couple of camping mattresses and sleeping bags. We can both sleep out under the stars.'

'Great,' I said.

Zach returned an hour later with some bedding, mossie nets, and a cool box. I led Asha into the enclosure and brought in her evening meal of a small antelope carcass, which she gnawed on hungrily.

We arranged the camping mats down on the ground next to each other in the middle of her enclosure.

Nodding to the cool box, I said, 'What's in there?'

'Cold beer.' He opened the lid and twisted off the cap of one bottle, handing it to me before taking one for himself. 'There's nothing quite like camping out here at night, watching the stars, with a cold beer. It doesn't get any better than this.' Zach stared at the sky and gave a satisfied sigh and took a swig of beer.

I turned my face up to the stars. There was no light pollution here so thousands of bright sparks lit up the sky, twinkling like diamonds. I remembered the luminous stars Mum had put on my ceiling at home and felt a pang of sadness that made me shiver. Had she done this with Dad when they lived out here? Enjoyed a cold beer as they stargazed up into the Kenyan night? Was her spirit closer to me here than in England?

'Are you cold?' Zach asked.

I shook my head, willing the lump in my throat to disappear.

'You're shivering. It can get cold out here at night.' He slipped an arm around me and rubbed my back.

The nerve endings in my body came alive, firing pulses in all directions. I took a small sip of beer, swirling the bitter liquid in my mouth before swallowing, so I wouldn't choke on it through either sadness or the shock of Zach's touch.

'It's nice beer,' I said.

'Is that the first time you've had beer?'

'I've had the odd swig of Dad's, but that's about it. What, are you going to tell me that you learned to drink beer at six years old, too?'

He tilted his head. 'No, not six. Seven, maybe.'

By the time Asha finished sucking the bones clean we were on our second bottle, and a relaxed feeling had settled in the pit of my stomach. Asha sat next to us and rested her head on her front paws, looking out through the iron bars of the enclosure into the black night at something I couldn't see.

'Where did the name Jazz come from?' Zach stopped rubbing my back and leaned on one arm, stretching out his long, toned legs.

'Mum absolutely loved jazz music. She had this massive collection of old vinyl records.' I smiled at the memory of her swaying her hips to the music as she cooked us dinner, or tapped her feet when she was curled up on the sofa reading a book. 'She kept trying to convert me, but I'm a pop girl. What about the name Zach?'

'Mum and Dad couldn't decide whether to call me something European or a Swahili name. Luckily the European name won, otherwise they'd have called me Kandoro.'

I laughed, then slapped a hand over my mouth. 'That's not so bad.'

'It means sweet potato.' He grinned.

'Oh.' I pulled a face at him.

His gaze swept over me for a while before he said, 'What happened in the accident?'

He hadn't asked me anything personal since that day at the lake when I'd stormed off, but suddenly I found myself actually wanting to tell him. Maybe it was the beer that made me more relaxed, or maybe it was that I was certain he wouldn't laugh at me anymore. It wasn't like I'd been able to hide my face from him in the last four months, and most of the time now, I didn't even think about wearing a hat or trying to covering my face with my hair when I was with him. I felt like I could trust him with my thoughts.

I swallowed some beer for courage. 'It was my fault.' I looked down at Asha and stroked her.

'How was it your fault?'

'I was running late for school, and Mum had been trying to hurry me up. We got in the car and half way there I realised I'd forgotten a text book I needed for an English exam, so we had to rush back and get it. As we drove off the second time around, I was telling Mum to go faster, and she was so busy telling me to put my seatbelt on that she wasn't paying attention to the road and drove through a red light.' I took a deep breath and shivered, suddenly feeling cold again in the warm air. 'A lorry ploughed into the driver's side and pushed us into a tree. She was crushed.' My voice cracked.

I felt his warm fingers slip around mine and he gave them a squeeze. 'Jazz–'

I cut him off and carried on talking, forcing the words out before I could change my mind. I hadn't spoken to anyone about what had happened, and now I had to get it all out of me. 'If it hadn't been for me being late and not wearing a seat belt, she'd still be alive.' The stars blurred in my vision as my eyes watered. 'I ended up going through the windscreen and landing on the mangled up bonnet, and I woke up in the hospital with my face ripped to shreds. I spent a few weeks in hospital and months going to the doctor to get the scars checked regularly.' I paused, remembering how I'd anticipated each appointment, imagining that the dressings would be uncovered and my face would be back to normal. The sense of loss, anger, and disappointment I felt when I realised they were still there in all their ugliness. 'I missed months of school, too. I used to hang around with a small group of the popular girls, and I had a best friend called Josie, but she was emigrating to Australia at that time with her parents. The others phoned me at first to see how I was getting on, but I think they just didn't know what to say to me. I mean, what do you say to someone who's lost their mum and is now scarred for life? And then, when the dressings were finally removed for good and they saw the state of me, one by one, they couldn't stand to be associated with me anymore. I mean, maybe some of it was my fault because I was so depressed. I didn't want to talk to anyone, and I was really angry all the time, but when I went back to school, that's when the teasing and name-calling started.'

I felt his hand squeeze mine tighter.

'I went from being in the popular crowd to being in the outcast crowd.'

'People think adults can be cruel, but kids are the worst,' Zach said.

'I know.' I paused. 'I couldn't stand to look at myself after that. Not only was I horrifically scarred, but I just felt so guilty about Mum. And I miss her so much.' I took a swig of beer to try and stop the tears from falling. 'Even now, and it's been nearly a year and a half. Does it ever get any easier?'

'There's no time limit on grief, but it does get easier.'

'I still talk to her. Does that sound weird?'

'Not at all.'

'I used to have a recurring dream about Mum, but it's strange; I stopped having it when I found Asha.' I leaned over to Asha and kissed the top of her head. She looked up at me and yawned.

'Asha's an amazing animal. You should be really proud of what you've done so far.'

'I haven't done that much.'

'I think you underestimate yourself.' He paused, tilting his head, thinking. 'You know…some people think scars are sexy. And I don't think your scars are as bad as you think they are.'

I gave him a disbelieving frown. He was just trying to make me feel better, and it wouldn't work.

'There are some African tribes who purposely scar their bodies and faces,' he went on.

I raised my eyebrows. 'What? Why on earth would they do that?'

'It's dying out a bit now, but it began because the climate here meant they were too hot to wear clothes so they would use scarring to recognise different tribes. It's also used to decorate and beautify the body. A bit like an ancient form of tattooing.'

Fathiya's comments about me being a long lost African child suddenly clicked into place. She wasn't being nasty, she'd just been making an observation.

'Look at the singer Seal,' he said. 'He's got facial scars, but I bet he's got a lot of female fans who find him sexy. Probably a few male ones, too.' He grinned as he reached out and wiped a tear away from my cheek with the back of his forefinger.

He looked deep into my eyes, and at that moment I understood what he'd said all those months ago, about not wanting to be anywhere else in the world other than here.

I felt like I'd finally come home.

Chapter 13

'Just pull it!' Zach shouted as he stood a little way in front, filming Asha and me.

I glanced down at the baby warthog carcass tied to a piece of rope and then looked back at Zach, scrunching up my face. 'She's not chasing it.' My shoulder slumped with frustration. I'd been running around for half an hour, trying to get her to chase it so she'd learn to associate a running animal with her food.

'She'll get the hang of it eventually.'

I sighed, wiping the sweat from my face, and ran off again, looking behind me at Asha, who seemed more concerned with a couple of zebra in the distance.

'Asha,' I called in a frustrated voice. 'Come on.'

'Just relax,' Zach called. 'You'll transfer your anxiety onto her.'

I huffed and stopped running.

Asha's head jerked up then and she started running, but not in my direction. She was heading towards a couple of hyenas trotting down into the valley in front of us.

Knowing that they could deliver a very nasty bite, I cried, 'Oh, no! Asha! Asha, come back.' I looked at Zach. 'What should we do?' I screeched.

He carried on filming her as she ran to within fifty metres of them. 'Just watch and see what happens. This is all part of her learning process.'

I watched with agonising anticipation of what would happen next.

The hyenas turned and fled back up the valley towards a hill on the other side with Asha chasing after them at great speed, her muscles rippling in the sunny haze. When the hyenas disappeared from view behind the hill Asha carried on until the white tip of her tail slipped over the horizon.

'Asha!' I cried, running towards where I'd last seen her.

'Jazz, come back!' Zach yelled behind me, and I heard his foot steps chasing after both of us.

I'd just got halfway to the hill when Asha reappeared, running back towards me at full speed.

I stopped, panting, relief flooding through me, and then I realised she wasn't alone. The hyenas were hot on her tail, chasing her back towards me.

I did an about turn and ran towards Zach as Asha shot past me and up the trunk of a nearby tree.

Zach waved his arms in the air, shouting at the hyenas, and they skidded to a halt, staring at us with wary eyes. I copied him, until we were both screaming at the top of our lungs, but they didn't show any signs of leaving. It wasn't until Zach fired a shot into the air that they ran away with their tails between their legs.

I leaned over, resting my hands on my knees, trying to get my breath back. 'Wow… that was…close.'

While Zach got on the radio to tell everyone he'd fired a shot, I glanced up at Asha, casually sitting in the tree, looking down at us with a haughty expression, as if to say, *What's all the fuss about?*

'Look at her.' I pointed to Asha. 'She's the one that gets us into trouble and then leaves us to it.'

'Looks like she's learning a valuable lesson. Her place of safety is always going to be in the trees, and that's exactly where she headed.'

I collapsed onto the ground to get my breath back. 'I don't think I can run any more.'

'Wimp,' he said.

'No, you're the wimp. You get a scratch and you're freaking out.'

He tutted. 'It was more than a scratch. You're never going to let me forget that, are you?'

'Nope.'

He strode towards me, grabbed hold of my hand, and pulled me to my feet. 'You can't stop now. Pull the warthog along and see if she chases it.'

I threw my hands in the air, faking my annoyance. 'You're a slave driver!' Slowly, I bent down and picked up the end of the rope before running off away from the tree, glancing over my shoulder at Asha.

Instantly, she was alert, and with a graceful leap from the tree she landed silently before sprinting towards the carcass. One fluid pounce and her front paws were holding it down on the ground. Her jaws locked around the warthog's neck, instinctively knowing the vital spot. After a few minutes with her practice stranglehold, Asha released the warthog, looking up at me for approval.

I jumped up and down with excitement. 'Good girl, Asha!' I stroked her head to praise her on a job well done, and she nuzzled into my hand proudly before turning her attention back to the warthog and tucking into the belly area where the hide was thinner and easier for her to penetrate with her teeth.

Zach turned the camera off and hurried towards me. Without thinking what I was doing, I threw my arms around his neck and launched myself towards him.

'She did it!' I cried, feeling his strong arms circle my waist. 'Did you get that on camera?'

'I did. Congratulations, Mum,' he said into my ear. 'But don't celebrate too soon. There's still a long way to go.'

I pulled back and slapped his arm playfully. 'Spoilsport.'

'I'm just being realistic. Soon, we'll have to try and get her to chase prey on a rope attached to the Land Rover. But the real test will be trying to get her to kill live prey. Some of the antelope run so fast she won't be able to keep up, and that's probably going to be a big source of her food. She's going to have to use her brain to survive out here.'

'Well, nothing's going to spoil my good mood.' I gave him a goofy grin. 'Asha deserves a medal for her part today.'

We'd been so distracted by Asha that we hadn't noticed

the dark clouds building up. A loud crack of thunder exploded above us just as the heavens opened and torrential rain poured down, soaking us within seconds. Zach fumbled around, trying to get the camera back in its case before it got ruined, and Asha huddled next to the warthog looking very annoyed at the wet interruption from her dinner.

As soon as Zach managed to put the camera away, he grabbed my hand and ran as the sky lit up with a lightning bolt. 'It doesn't look like this is going to let up, and there's a cave a bit further up here,' he shouted over the noise of the thunder and rain. 'We can shelter until it stops.'

'Come on, Asha,' I called to her to follow. She was of the same opinion as us and didn't need much encouragement to get out of the nasty weather, but there was no way she was leaving her warthog behind. She dragged it between her front paws until we arrived at the base of some large rocks.

Zach pointed to the cave above us. 'I need to make sure there aren't any other animals sheltering in there before you go up. Wouldn't want to stumble on a leopard or a snake. Stay here.' He climbed up the side of the rocks and looked inside before beckoning me to follow.

I climbed up with ease and Asha followed, dragging her carcass up the rocks and starting to feed.

Pulling the soaking wet T-shirt away from my skin, I wafted it about, feeling conscious that it was now pretty see-through. Zach's shirt and shorts were moulded to his body, too. I sat down next to him as Asha shook herself and water flew all over us.

'Hey!' I cried at her, wrapping my arms around me and shivering at the sudden drop in temperature.

Zach looked at my clothes. 'You should probably take them off, if you want to stay warm.'

I gawped at him. My body was reacting strangely enough around him lately without me taking my clothes off, too.

He laughed at my expression and shrugged. 'You'll feel the cold more if your clothes are wet.'

'Why aren't you taking your clothes off, then?' I smirked.

'Because I'm not the one shivering to death.'

I wrapped my arms around me, rubbing my hands up and down to try and keep warm, and felt Zach's arm slide around my shoulders and pull me closer.

He was right. His body was still like a furnace. He rubbed up and down my back and I felt myself melting under his touch. I looked at him out of the corner of my eye, wondering what he was thinking. Did he feel the same things I'd been feeling when we touched, or was he just being a good friend to me? That was Zach all over – sensitive, kind, passionate about wildlife, an all round Mr Nice Guy.

'The rainy season's started.' He stared out of the cave, oblivious to the turmoil of thoughts buzzing in my head.

The raindrops sliced noisily through the air like missiles, saturating the ground and forming small gullies that flowed towards the river. It was coming down so hard you could barely see a metre in front of you.

'Within a few weeks there'll be new vegetation growing and an abundance of grazing animals back in the Masai Mara Reserve. New animals will be born, closely followed by more predators. These rains contribute to the endless cycle of nature out here. It's kind of like wiping the slate clean and starting all over again.'

I bit my lip, twisting a strand of hair round my finger. How good would it feel to wipe my slate clean and start over?

'I'd better head out to see Kira tomorrow before the weather gets worse,' he said.

Kira. Of course.

I felt like I'd been kicked in the chest. When there was someone as gorgeous as Kira around, I'd never be able to compete. What an idiot I'd been for even thinking something could ever happen between us. How could he possibly fall in love with me when he could have the choice of any beautiful woman he wanted?

One thing was certain. I would never be able to tell him how I felt.

Chapter 14

'I've had some amazing news.' Zach rushed up to me one morning. 'One of the American national newspapers heard about what you're doing with Asha and wants to come out and run a story on it.' His grin lit up his whole face.

'That's fantastic.' I smiled back. 'The more stories there are about poaching, the more the message will get out that it needs to be stopped.'

'So you'll do an interview with them?'

I frowned, pointing to my chest. 'Me? You know more about the technical side of poaching than me. Surely you'd be better at it.' A feeling of dread froze my spine. It was one thing to be more comfortable with my appearance in front of Zach, but a reporter? What if they said something horrible about my face? I could imagine the headlines: *Beauty and the Beast.* Except Asha would be the beauty and I'd be the beast. I'd be the object of so much ridicule and laughter.

I shook my head. 'No, you do it.'

Disappointment clouded his face. 'But they want to interview you. You're the one working with Asha. You're the one making it possible.'

'I…I don't know.'

He gazed at me seriously. 'You said it yourself. We need to raise awareness about anti-poaching and conservation, and this publicity can only help.' He glanced at Asha in her enclosure, her paws twitching with excitement, grumbling to be let out for her morning walk. 'Do it for Asha.'

I gnawed on my fingernail.

He was right. This was Asha's story and it needed to be told. 'I don't want them to take any photos of my face,' I said.

'They probably will want to take some photos.' He pursed his lips, trying to come up with a solution. 'Maybe we can give them a shot of you and Asha from behind.'

'But what am I going to say?' I whined. 'I don't want to sound like an idiot in the papers.'

'Have faith in yourself, Jazz. Just speak from the heart about it. That's all you can do.'

But that was easier said than done. What did I know about being interviewed? And this was such a serious subject that I wanted to do it justice. I couldn't bear the thought of more animals being slaughtered.

For the next few weeks until the journalist arrived I quizzed Zach, Dad, and Richard about poaching and was consumed with worry about it as I tried to come up with possible questions in my head that they might ask and my possible answers.

Her name was Rebecca Swanson, and she arrived at the lodge one afternoon. There was a flurry of excitement over there, but I kept away from it all. Apart from doing the interview, it was probably better for me to have as little to do with her as possible. I didn't want to mess it up by her taking a dislike to me because of how I looked.

She spent the first day out on the reserve with Richard and Dad to get a feel for Kilingi, and the next day she went into Jito so she could talk to the local villagers. On the third day I heard them arrive outside our quarters in the Land Rover and wiped my sweating palms down the back of my shorts, peering out of the kitchen window. She was in her early thirties, with a sleek-cut black bob, cheekbones so sharp they could cut glass, and perfectly shaped eyebrows. She looked fresh in a white linen trouser suit with luscious red lipstick and nails that screamed of a polished, no-nonsense career woman. She had a camera strapped around her neck and was carrying a notebook and handheld recorder.

Zach leaped up the stairs two at a time while Richard and Dad led her to Asha's enclosure. Asha watched them tentatively from the back fence. She could tell instinctively whether someone liked her or not and she wouldn't come closer to the fence, despite Dad's coaxing.

'She's here.' Zach came into the kitchen.

'Is she nice?' I carried on staring through the window, knees feeling like jelly.

'Yes. She seems very nice. Come on, she's only here for one more night and she wants to get started.' Seeing the panic that must've been obvious on my face, he strode towards me. 'You can do this. It'll be fine.'

I thought about Asha and how she trusted me to be her mum. I was going to have to be her advocate, and the advocate for all the animals out there who didn't have a voice. This article had the potential to help raise awareness about how devastating and abhorrent poaching was, and the weight of it sat heavily on my shoulders.

I sucked in a huge breath and nodded, slowly following him outside.

'Here she is,' Zach said to them, and the group turned to look at me.

Dad and Richard smiled, but Rebecca wasn't quick enough to hide the surprise on her face at my appearance. She stood there staring for a moment, eyes wide with an expression of horror, before she realised what she was doing and cleared her throat.

I cringed inwardly.

'Rebecca Swanson.' She held her hand out to shake mine. 'Nice…to…meet…you,' she pronounced the words very slowly, as if I was deaf, and plastered a smile on her face.

It wasn't the first time that someone thought I might have some kind of mental slowness because of the way I looked, but it still got to me. I caught Zach's eye, and he gave me a pained look.

Shaking her hand, I felt a hot red rash creep up my neck. 'Jazz Hooper. Nice to meet you, too,' my voice came out hoarse.

'I'd…like…to…get…a…few…shots…of…Asha…first,'

she said.

'It's OK, I'm not deaf,' I blurted out.

Her eyes flashed wide for a second in surprise and then, realising her mistake, she regained her composure and ran a hand through her hair, straightening up her back and turning towards Asha. 'OK, let's get started, then,' she said in a brusque voice. 'Let me just get a few shots of her in the enclosure and then we'll do the interview.'

I avoided everyone's gaze and mumbled, 'OK,' then shuffled uncomfortably from one foot to the other until she finished.

'Can we sit up there in the shade?' Rebecca nodded her head towards the veranda after she got her photos.

'Of course,' Dad said. 'Do you want a cold drink while you're working?' he asked Rebecca.

She gave him a blood-red smile. 'That would be lovely.' And she stalked towards the veranda.

I shuffled behind the group and felt Zach reach for my hand and squeeze it. 'You'll be fine, don't worry,' he whispered.

I sat down opposite Rebecca as Richard, Dad, and Zach disappeared inside the house. She set her notebook on her knees, pulled a pen out of the centre binding, and put the voice recorder on the table. 'Do you mind if I record this interview while I take notes?' She gave me a scrutinising gaze.

I shook my head softly and felt the hair on my scalp prickling under her eyes. I stared at the ground. 'Er...no.'

'Here we are; homemade lemonade.' Dad placed a glass in front of Rebecca and handed me one.

'Fantastic,' Rebecca said.

'Jazz made it,' he said with a proud grin.

She took a sip. 'Lovely.' Setting it back down, she tapped her pen on her notebook. 'Right, let's get to work.'

Dad disappeared and left us to it.

Rebecca pressed the *play* button on the recorder and said, 'So, tell me about Asha. What happened to her mother?'

'She…she was killed by poachers.'

She nodded and waved a hand in front of her in a *go on* gesture.

'Um…it seems to be happening more and more now. There are small-time poachers who kill the animals for food, but there are also gangs of professionals who kill them for all kind of things like their skins, horns, ivory, bones—'

'Yes, and who were these poachers?' she interrupted me.

'We don't know. They got away. But these days there are well-organized, international gangs of poachers and traffickers in the illegal wildlife trade.'

She pointed her pen around the area. 'And what do the local people think about this?'

'I'm sorry, I don't know what you mean,' I said.

She raised a perfectly shaped eyebrow. 'Well, some of the villagers and settlements I visited yesterday are very poor. They told me that they have a right to hunt animals for food or to protect their livestock from predators. If they're unable to do that, their livelihoods will be affected, won't they?'

'Yes, some people do feel like that, but we need to educate the local people about co-existing with the wildlife, not destroying it. The game reserves in the area actually provide employment for local people.'

She made of note of something on her pad. 'What sort of education are you talking about?'

'Er…I don't know, exactly, but—'

She cut me off. 'Well, the villagers and tribes were here long before the establishment of the game reserves. Do you think we should put the animals' rights before the rights of the local people?'

'I just know that this kind of poaching can't keep happening,' I carried on. 'The black rhino, for example, is critically endangered and will be extinct in the near future if the poaching continues. Tigers are being wiped out because of Asian medicine, with only around five hundred left of certain species. There are less than forty Amur leopards left in the world. The African leopard is listed as "near threatened" and they're becoming more rare outside of protected areas. If this carries on, they'll become endangered, too. In the sixties, over fifty thousand leopards were being killed each year in Africa for their fur.' My voice rose with passion. 'Some animal parts are worth more than gold to these people.'

Swiftly changing the subject, she asked, 'So what are you doing to get Asha ready for release into the game reserve?'

I wiped my palms on my thighs. 'Well, I'm trying to teach her everything she'll need to know to be a fully functioning wild leopard. She's seven months old now, and she's doing really well so far. I've introduced her to different kinds of prey, since leopards have a very varied diet, and soon we'll be teaching her to chase carcasses from the back of a Land Rover to get her used to chasing her kills.'

'Then what?'

'We'll have to introduce live prey to her.'

She grimaced. 'And what will that be?'

'Things like impala, antelope, warthogs, birds, fish.'

'You must have a strong stomach.'

I picked at my fingernail. 'Well, it's not something I'd normally choose to do. Taking on the role of her mother means dealing with the good things and the bad. It's essential for her survival because if she doesn't learn to hunt, she'll never be released. It's better to teach her that than have her in a zoo somewhere with no freedom.'

'Aren't you worried that she'll become too used to humans?'

'Her contact is limited to me and Zach. Dad will only have contact with her if she needs any veterinary care. And people who stay at the lodge aren't allowed out here to see her.' I paused. 'There is a risk that she'll get too used to humans, but it's a risk that we have to take to get her to the stage where she can be released.'

She frowned. 'I've heard of incidents where animals have been re-wilded and released and then gone on to attack humans.'

'I think that when a wild animal gets used to humans, if they see them out in their habitat, they'll often go towards them instead of away from them. Then, of course, the people run away, but the running triggers the animal's hunting instincts and they chase them. Towards the end of Asha's re-wilding I'll have to cut off most of my contact with her.' A sad feeling drifted over me, dreading that day. Asha had been my life since we'd arrived in Kenya, and even though we had a long way to go, I couldn't imagine not being with her every day.

She carried on asking me questions for another three quarters of an hour and then slid her pen in the spine of the notebook and turned off the recorder. She stood and shook my hand. 'Thank you.' She paused for a moment, head tilted, a sympathetic look on her face. 'What do you think should happen to these poachers?'

'Maybe they should have a taste of their own medicine.'

'What do you mean?'

'Well, how would they like to be shot and mutilated? Some rhinos have their horns hacked off while they're still alive and are just left for dead.'

'Poaching is a crime here, isn't it? Why not just leave it to the authorities?'

'It is a crime, but catching them is another matter. They're armed and very dangerous. Plus, even if they're caught, the punishment is so minimal it makes no difference to them.'

'I see.' She nodded thoughtfully and we walked towards the steps. 'So, do you think that the villagers shouldn't be allowed to have firearms out here, then?'

'Well, I guess some may need them for protection if they use the National Parks to graze their livestock or work with animals, but no, I don't think most people should have them at all.'

Richard and Dad came out to take her back to the lodge and Zach stayed behind.

'How did it go?' he asked.

'Er...OK, I think. I was so nervous!' I went over the

questions she'd asked me and what I could remember of my answers, but my brain was in such a scramble I'd forgotten most of what I'd said.

'I'm sure you did great. Rebecca says they'll be running the piece in the Saturday supplement.' He grinned. 'I'm really proud of you.'

I felt a hot blush sweeping over my cheeks. Fingers crossed I'd said all the right things.

On Saturday I crept into the office at the lodge to send an email to Aunt Katrina when I knew the guests would be out on safari. I regularly filled her in on what I'd been doing with Asha now, and, as always, her replies were encouraging and fun. As I tapped away on the keyboard, I heard Dad and Zach's voices in quiet conversation out in reception.

'You can't tell Jazz,' Dad said firmly.

'We have to. She knows the piece is due out today; she'll be asking about it.'

'I can't believe Rebecca wrote that,' Dad said. 'She seemed very interested and sympathetic to anti-poaching when she was here.'

'I know. There's no way Jazz would've said something like that.'

I leaped out of the chair and rushed out to reception. 'What are you talking about?'

Zach gave Dad a sheepish look.

'What's happened?' I asked, flapping my hand to get them to hurry up and tell me.

Dad held a copy of Rebecca's article that he'd printed from their webpage in his hand.

I felt the blood rising to the surface. 'Just tell me!'

Dad said, 'The article is pro-hunting, and she's called you an anti-gun fascist!'

'What do you mean?' I snatched it out of his hands and started reading...

Animal Rights Advocate is an Anti-Gun Fascist!

Once again, the question of hunting rears its head, and here's a fact that the animal rights crowd don't like admitting: We wouldn't have nearly as much publicly owned land to enjoy our outdoor life of walking, biking, horse-riding, etc if it weren't for hunters spending thousands of dollars on license fees, permits, and equipment.

Wild animals, and especially endangered or threatened species, are much better off by having thousands of miles of patrolled habitat that these dollars are paying for than the propaganda and half-truths that the animal rights groups dish out. If hunting were banned, where would the money for preservation actually come from to increase habitat for game species? And what about the rights of the Africans to earn their living? That would all disappear overnight. It seems to me that rich white hypocrisy is in play here, allowing people to dote on animals while leaving the poor villagers without a livelihood. Whether you want to admit it or not, the huge amount of sportsmen's money pumped into hunting has contributed to the re-establishment of certain species and to wildlife conservation, and provides much-needed economy for the local villagers. Who else could pay for the upkeep of these public lands? The animal rights activists? I think not.

Jazz Hooper is an animal rights advocate who thinks differently. I met her in Kenya recently after hearing how she'd found a leopard cub whose mother, she claimed, had been shot by hunters, and she's rearing it to be released back into the Kilingi Game Reserve. If Jazz had her way, everyone in Africa, and especially uneducated people, should be stripped of their right to bear arms, making her nothing but an anti-gun fascist. This...

I couldn't read the rest of the article. I looked up at them both with horror. 'But that's not what I said! She's completely twisted everything.' I wracked my brains, trying to remember exactly what I had said.

'We didn't think you would,' Zach said, shaking his head.

'But I didn't even mention hunting. I was talking poaching and the illegal wildlife trade,' I said.

'She obviously hasn't done any research into hunting, either,' Zach said. 'If she had, she'd mention the canned lion hunts, where they're bred in captivity and drugged before being released so some rich guy with a gun can inflate his ego by shooting it and taking home a trophy to stuff. Or about the pseudo rhino hunts, where the Vietnamese can get a permit to shoot a rhino on a game farm and then export the horn as a so-called "trophy", but really it's destined to be ground up into Eastern medicine. Rhino are so shortsighted that if you're downwind of them, they wouldn't even know you were there. These animals are easy to kill. How is shooting an animal that has no chance against a gun a "sport"?' He blew out an angry breath. 'There's really no difference between hunting and poaching; they're both murder. It's just that hunting is a legalised version.'

'She's talking about the animal rights groups, but what animal rights? They don't have any!' Dad spat. 'It's a totally unprofessional article and no doubt she's been paid off by the powerful pro-hunting, pro-gun lobbyists.'

'I remember saying that people needed to be educated about poaching. And then…' I paced up and down, thinking. 'She asked me something at the end about what should happen to the poachers and I said maybe they should have a taste of their own medicine. And I told her about animals having their horns mutilated when they were still alive.' I threw my hands up in the air.

'Bloody newspapers,' Dad tutted.

I looked down and started reading again, my eyes frantically scanning the page. 'What can we do?' I asked urgently. 'It looks terrible. And it's completely biased.'

Zach and Dad exchanged a worried glance.

'What?' I questioned them.

'Since the name of the reserve is mentioned in the article, we've already had hundreds of emails complaining about your alleged remarks. And the pro-hunting, pro-gun groups are up in arms over it. We've even had some threats,' Zach said.

I collapsed onto the leather sofa in the centre of reception. 'But I didn't say it like that!' I wailed. 'I didn't mean for any of this to happen.'

'We can try and get them to print a retraction,' Zach suggested to Dad.

'Yes, but that will just be a small statement with tiny lettering in an obscure part of the paper that no one actually sees.' Dad sighed.

Zach ran a hand over his cropped hair. 'It's already doing the rounds on social media. It's gone viral. Everyone's talking about it.'

I flopped my head forward and tugged at my hair. 'I thought I was trying to do something to help, and now I've ruined everything, as usual.'

'It will blow over eventually,' Zach said. 'They'll find some other poor person to misquote and move onto that. Today's news is tomorrow's chip wrappers.'

'But what about in the meantime?' I asked from behind my hair. 'I never meant to do anything to jeopardise the reserve or Asha.'

Dad sat down next to me and put his arm round my shoulder, pulling me towards him. 'We know that, sweetheart. It's not your fault.'

'And anyway, poachers do deserve to have a taste of their own medicine,' Zach said. 'Except that wouldn't really stop anything. There are plenty of people in Africa living in poverty who would do anything for the amount of money they're being offered by these big crime syndicates to poach. The only way to stop it is to get the people at the top and eliminate the market for it.'

'I bet that woman is walking around in a leopard skin coat and mink slippers, but I doubt she's looked at one skinned with its paws and head cut off.' Dad sat down on the other side of me. 'People don't realise what it's like out here. We're the only things that stand between the poachers and those animals. If we don't try and ensure conservation, what's going to happen to them?'

I knew he was trying to make me feel better, but it wasn't working.

Dad stood up. 'I'd better go and break the news to Jenna and Richard.'

As I heard his footsteps disappear into the distance, Zach grabbed my hand and pulled me to my feet. 'Come on. I want to show you something.' He dragged me out the door.

'Where are we going?' All I wanted was to be left alone to wallow in self-pity. I'd stuffed everything up without even trying. I wasn't just an ugly freak. I was now an ugly idiot.

He pulled me along the track that led to our quarters and marched me up to Asha's enclosure. On seeing us, she trotted up to the bars and pushed her nose through the gap, excited to see me.

'What are we doing here?' I moaned.

'Look at her.'

I stroked under her chin as she mewed in her leopard chat appreciation.

'There's one thing that always amazes me about animals,' he said. 'They never show unkindness. They show a lot of other human traits like love and kindness, compassion, fear, anger, and yes, there are animals that kill each other. Either they hunt to feed or they defend their young to the death, but they never do anything without a good reason. When I was out in the reserve once I witnessed something amazing. We were watching Big Mama's herd grazing. A lone male elephant arrived that had its trunk caught in a poacher's wire noose-snare and couldn't use it to pick up food. It walked up to Big Mama and showed her its trunk. Knowing the injured elephant needed help, Big Mama uprooted a small acacia tree and picked off some leaves, putting them straight into the injured one's mouth.' He glanced at me. 'There are many stories of disabled animals instinctively being fed and cared for and helped out by their family. Blind animals being protected by their herd. Predators befriending prey animals and actually hanging out with them. Swimmers being saved by dolphins. Some of them could teach humans a thing or two about compassion and kindness, and some of them make better parents than some humans. We could learn a lot from them because I think deliberate cruelty is only found in the human race.' He paused. 'That woman had her own agenda when she was writing that story, and it was never about Asha. She just wanted to sensationalise something so she could sell more papers.' He pointed at Asha. '*She's* the reason we're doing this, and don't ever let anything make you forget that.'

Chapter 15

I woke up early, as usual, and listened to the sounds of the African plains coming to life. Birds sang their early morning chorus, and in the distance I could hear elephants trumpeting in the new day.

Our first Christmas Day in Kenya. Another Christmas without Mum.

I stared at her photo, thinking about how she'd always left a stocking outside my door with little knick-knacky presents in it. Hair clips, nuts, socks, a book, a satsuma. I still thought about her every day and talked to her constantly in my head. I wondered what she'd think of me now. I'd thought I was doing something worthwhile with Asha, but I still had the ability to ruin everything and mess up people's lives. They weren't little things, either; inconsequential mistakes that didn't hurt anyone. When I stuffed up, I did it in style. Mum's death just proved that, and now people cancelling their holidays with the reserve after that horrible story had run just confirmed it.

I rolled onto my side and stared through the window, not wanting to get out of bed. Maybe I could just stay here all day with the covers pulled over my head. Would anyone even notice? It wasn't like I was much good for anything, was I?

Dad knocked on my door a while later. 'Happy Christmas, sweetheart. I've brought you some tea.' He opened the door, his eyebrows pinching together when he saw my face. Putting the mug down on the bedside table, he sat on the bed next to me. 'Come on, get up. Asha needs feeding.'

'I still miss her,' I said, staring at the steam coming off the mug.

He reached out and squeezed my shoulder. 'Me, too. Every day. But it's important to think about all the time we *did* have together. Some people don't even get that. Just because she's not here anymore, doesn't mean she's not with you. She's in our hearts, and nothing and no one can change that. She'd be really proud of you, you know.'

I snorted. 'How do you work that out?'

'Since we got here, I've seen you blossoming for the first time since the accident. Whether you believe it or not, I can tell you that you've grown into a strong young lady.'

I gave him a disbelieving look.

'You've had a rough time of it. We both have. There will always be setbacks and knocks in life, you can't control that, and you can't be responsible for everything that happens. I don't know many sixteen-year-olds who are doing what you're doing with such passion.' He smiled softly and stood up. 'Yes, it's Christmas Day, and it's not the same without your mum, but Asha still needs feeding and walking, I've still got animals to care for, and you still have to get out of bed. Life has to go on.'

Groaning, I sat up and drank my tea as Dad left me to get dressed.

When I went outside to Asha's enclosure, she was hiding in one of the thickets, and I knew she was about to ambush me, which was something she'd started doing on a regular basis.

I opened the door and stepped inside, pretending I hadn't seen her bum and tail sticking out of the other side of the bush as I walked slowly past. I knew when she was about to pounce because her tail always twitched slightly.

I could feel her eyes on me and watched her rear end closely. When her tail twitched, I jumped out of reach, laughing.

She didn't let me get one over on her, though, deciding to launch herself onto me with excitement. She didn't know her own strength anymore and knocked me to the ground. Within seconds we were rolling about, playing, and I felt my mood lift slightly. Her trusting nature and energetic personality had the ability to make everything seem brighter. Maybe Dad was right. Maybe Mum would've been proud of me.

I grabbed her tail and gave it a gentle tug, quickly moving my hand away before she could swat me with her paw. It kept her entertained for hours, and eventually, when we were both worn out, I said, 'I bet you want your breakfast, don't you?' I sat up, covered in dust, and hugged her towards me. She licked my arm in reply.

Zach walked up to the enclosure with a smile on his face. 'Happy Christmas.'

I mustered up a feeble smile. 'Happy Christmas.'

'And how are you two girls doing?'

'OK, I suppose.'

'I thought we could give Asha a Christmas present,' he said, holding up a small gazelle carcass.

I pulled a face at it. I still hated giving her carcasses.

'You're so lazy that you don't run fast enough to give her any challenge to catch her dinner, so we need to attach it to the Land Rover and get her to chase it.' He grinned.

I narrowed my eyes at him. 'I'm not lazy!'

'Well, prove it, then. Stop playing around and let's do some real work with her.'

I stood up, dusted myself off, and then slipped out of the door before Asha could follow me. If she saw the carcass she'd be scoffing it down before we had the chance to teach her anything.

While Zach lifted the dead animal onto a tarpaulin on the back of the Land Rover, I went inside to fetch some drinks and put them in a cool box. When the carcass was carefully wrapped up, I let Asha out and got into the passenger seat. She jumped in on top of me, but she was now so big that I ended up squirming out of the way and was perched on a tiny edge of it while she had the rest, sitting up like a queen of the manor, watching the world pass by with interest.

We drove for half an hour, and as we pulled round a corner

of thick bush a huge bull elephant stood in the middle of the track, his looming body blocking the way.

Zach skidded to a halt.

The elephant stared at us menacingly, flapping his ears and swinging his trunk.

I felt Asha's muscles tense in the seat next to me.

'Shit.' Zach put the Land Rover in reverse. 'That's Mr Grumpy and he's in musth, which means he's looking to mate. They've got so much testosterone flying through their body, they're unpredictable and dangerous. They've only got one thing on their minds, and that's the females.' He slowly eased the Land Rover backwards. 'He's pretty grumpy at the best of times, which is why we called him that, but he'll be even worse now. I don't want to move too suddenly, it might set him off.'

I kept my eyes on the bull as the Land Rover rolled back. Mr Grumpy lowered his head, lifted up a front leg, and barrelled forwards.

My stomach rose to my throat. 'He's charging us!'

Zach pushed the accelerator harder and the Land Rover lurched backwards.

Mr Grumpy's huge, hulking body stopped suddenly and he raised his trunk in the air with an angry trumpeting sound.

'It's a mock charge.' Zach swung the Land Rover around.' He just wants us out of his way so he can find the females.'

Mr Grumpy swayed backwards, as if giving himself enough room to charge forward again.

'Well get out of the way, then!' I cried.

'I'm trying!' Zach floored the Land Rover in the direction we'd just come, and I stared at Mr Grumpy over my shoulder.

My hand flew to my chest. 'He's stopped, thank God. He's just watching us now.'

Zach shook his head. 'If he'd really wanted to charge us, we'd just be like a little Tonka Toy in this thing.' He exhaled a huge breath of relief.

'That was really close!'

'You could've fired a warning shot in the air as I was driving,' Zach said.

'Well, why didn't you tell me?'

'I'm not always going to be around to tell you everything. Sometimes out here you're going to have to learn to use your initiative. Anyway, I was too busy driving.' He grinned as the relief hit us.

'I think it's kind of romantic that he's prepared to do anything to get a girlfriend,' I said.

'Yeah, as long as he doesn't kill us in the process.' Zach raised an eyebrow and drove on until we headed down a dirt track in between long grasses and had to stop to let a large African rock python slither across the path, going leisurely about its day. Out of the long grasses a cheetah poked its head out and looked at us.

'That's Kimani,' Zach said quietly. 'She was found by some farmers as an orphan and re-wilded by the Cheetah Conservation Organization and released here a couple of years ago. She loves coming up to the Land Rovers, and she's a real favourite with the guests.'

We watched as she began to approach the Land Rover then stopped when she spotted Asha.

Asha watched her warily, eyes alert, fidgeting in the seat and trying to work out whether to be scared, jump out and play, or go on the defensive.

'It's OK, Asha.' I held her collar firmly as she struggled to clamber over me and escape through the open window.

Kimani stared warily at Asha, her body frozen.

'Amazing, isn't she?' Zach nodded at Kimani. 'If Asha wasn't here, she'd be rubbing herself against the Land Rover, and sometimes she even jumps up on the bonnet.'

Asha made a low sound in her throat, struggling to get away from my tight grip on her collar.

Kimani bolted back into the grass.

'That will be you one day, Asha.' I kissed the top of her head. 'Living out here all the time, patrolling your kingdom.'

We eventually parked at a secluded spot and Zach jumped

out and tied the gazelle to the tow bar with a thick piece of rope. 'OK, let her out now,' he called. 'Make sure she sees the meat and then hop back in and I'll take off.'

Asha was already dying to get out. Her head bobbed up and down and she made excited mewing sounds. Her ears flicked, taking in all the sounds of the bush. As soon as I opened my door she jumped down and looked around her, head upturned, opening her mouth to scent the air.

'Look, Asha.' I walked to the back of the Land Rover and she spotted her dinner. Immediately, she went for it, and I ran around and jumped in the passenger seat. 'Go,' I yelled.

Zach drove off as I twisted in the seat to watch Asha. She stared at us with big, worried amber eyes, like we were leaving her there forever.

'Come on, Asha, chase it!' I called out the window.

That was the encouragement she needed and she was off, chasing the kill like she'd never been fed.

'It's working. She's chasing it.' I grinned at Zach, who was busy staring in front of him, trying to avoid too many bumps in the track.

'I've got to get this on film next time,' he breathed with excitement. 'This is fantastic. If we get her used to chasing her food, she should be able to chase live prey.'

As I watched her sprint closer to the gazelle, her hunting instinct must've taken over and she pounced on top of it, claws dug in for dear life, riding on top of the carcass.

'Stop!' I told Zach breathlessly. 'She's got it.'

He screeched to a halt.

Panting away, Asha had the dead animal by the throat in a choke hold. After a few minutes, she lifted her head up and looked at me through the rear window, as if to say, *Did I do good?*

'That was amazing.' I threw my arms around Zach's neck, caught up in the spirit of celebration. 'She did it. I can't believe it. She did it. Did you see how she got it round the throat? I think she's going to be a natural hunter.'

He pulled back to arm's length and grinned back. 'I bet

you don't get a Christmas present like that every day, eh?'

'Thank you,' I sang happily, turning round again to watch Asha feeding with relish, making low mumbling sounds as she ate.

'Are you coming up to the kitchen for Christmas dinner later?' Zach asked me. 'I've got a present for you.'

'Where did you get a present from out here? It's not exactly Oxford Street.' I smiled, feeling a little excited.

A present? For me? We were in the middle of the African bush. What on earth could he have got me? And it wasn't like I'd been thinking about presents, either. I just wanted to forget it was Christmas, but that was pretty hard to do because Richard and Jenna had gone overboard at the lodge, decorating a huge tree and playing Christmas carols for the guests who were staying during the festive period.

He tapped his nose and raised his eyebrow. 'You'll have to come to dinner and you'll find out.'

'But I can't go over there. Richard and Jenna must hate me after that article in the paper.' I'd been keeping an even lower profile than usual since Rebecca's horrible story broke, and I hadn't been up to the lodge in the last few weeks, afraid of what they would think of me.

'They don't hate you. It's not your fault that Rebecca manipulated what you said. And anyway, Kilingi has a good enough reputation to bounce back. Bookings are up for next year now.'

'I don't know,' I said, my thoughts drifting back to Mum. 'I don't feel up to a party.'

'It's not a party. It's just a group of friends and co-workers eating lunch. No big deal.' He shrugged. 'And the present will be worth it.' He bumped his shoulder against mine.

'OK,' I agreed reluctantly.

Later that afternoon I showered and changed into a black sundress. If we were going to have Christmas dinner, I thought I may as well try and get dressed in something other than my usual shorts and T-shirt. As I met Dad in the hall emerging from his bedroom, my breath caught in my throat. It didn't feel right celebrating. For one thing, Mum wasn't with us, and for another, I couldn't shake the feeling that Jenna and Richard wouldn't really want me there. Not that they'd ever been anything less than warm and friendly to me, but how could they not blame me for that article, despite what Zach said?

But when I saw my sadness reflected on Dad's face, I realised I had to go for him. He'd been working so hard, and even though he always put on a brave face for me, I knew he was still missing Mum deeply. He should be surrounded by his friends and what was left of his family without having to worry about how I was feeling.

He took hold of my hand and squeezed it. 'Ready?'

I nodded.

We slipped in the back door of the kitchen and some of the rangers and anti-poaching patrols were already there, enjoying a cold beer. Everyone called out Christmas greetings as Chef prepared steaming pots of vegetables, and the smell of roasting turkey made my stomach rumble.

Jenna enveloped me in a big hug. 'Lovely to see you, Jazz.'

'I'm really sorry about that—' I started, but she cut me off with a wave of her hand.

'Now, don't you go worrying about that. We know it wasn't your fault. And anyway,' she raised an eyebrow, 'what goes around, comes around. That Rebecca Swanson will get her comeuppance one day.' She let me go and kissed Dad on the cheek.

'Where's Bobo?' I asked.

'She's having a nap. She's been pigging out on bananas all day.' She chuckled.

'Happy Christmas.' Richard handed Dad a bottle of beer, which he took and chinked the glass against Richard's half empty one.

'Want a beer?' Richard said to me.

'I think she's old enough for a couple.' Dad winked at me.

'It is Christmas, after all.'

'Be right back,' Richard said.

I wandered away from everyone, over to Chef. 'It smells lovely. Can I do anything to help?'

He smiled, his eyes crinkling at the edges. 'It's roast leopard.' He cackled at the joke he thought was funny.

I poked him on the arm. 'Hey, that's not funny.'

'I thought it was.' He shrugged with his huge permanent grin plastered all over his face. 'Can you pass me those bowls? I'm about to serve everything up. Then I have to do it all again later for the guests. I never want to see another sprout in my life!' He shook his head good-naturedly and drained a pan of sprouts. 'Maybe the guests will like roast leopard,' he muttered.

I gave him a fake glare and helped dish up the vegetables and carry them to the long table as Zach appeared, freshly showered and shaven and dressed in faded jeans and a white shirt that set off his bronzed skin and jet black hair.

As he glanced at me and smiled, my insides tingled. Maybe it was the effects of the beer.

We all helped ourselves to food and I sat back, chewing slowly and watching everyone chat in an easy conversation, remembering the time I'd eaten here when we first arrived and had gone running out. So much had happened since then, and even though I still desperately wished Mum was sitting here with us, I was actually starting to feel glad to be in that steamy kitchen, watching them all enjoying being with each other.

'OK, I've got a big announcement to make.' Richard looked round the table. 'We've finally got the go ahead for the rhino release.'

'Really? When?' Dad looked up, all ears.

'I'm not sure yet, but I'll let you know as soon as all the details get finalised.'

'What's this?' I asked Dad

Dad rested his knife and fork on his plate. 'There are some black rhino in a game reserve in South Africa that are being relocated here for a breeding programme. There are only around three and a half thousand black rhino left in the world now. In the sixties there were seventy thousand.' He shook his head sadly. 'We're hoping this programme can help to increase the numbers.'

'Three and a half thousand?' I balked at the low numbers. The more time I spent here, the more I realised how sad it was what humans were capable of doing to wild animals.

'Thousands of rhinos have been killed, and subspecies have been hunted to extinction.' Richard shook his head. 'At least one rhino is killed every day in Africa by poachers, and the numbers are increasing every year.'

'The breeding programme is the best Christmas present I could've asked for, and I think that calls for a toast, don't you?' Dad tapped his spoon against his beer bottle and held it up in the air. 'To the rhino breeding programme.'

We all held our bottles in the air.

After dinner, I helped Jenna and Chef clear the tables and load up the industrial-sized dishwasher. I turned around to find Zach behind me.

'How about I give you your Christmas present now.' He held out a gift about the size of a book, wrapped up in decorative paper.

'Is it a book?' I took it. 'I need a new one. I have to make do with whatever the guests leave behind.'

His eyes glinted with mischief. 'Open it and find out.'

I unwrapped the paper. It was a photograph in a wooden frame of Asha and me that he must've taken when I wasn't looking. I was sitting on a mound of rocks, facing away from the camera, and Asha sat in front of me as I stroked her neck. It was so heartfelt and simple. A million times better than a new pair of shoes or the latest mobile phone that I would've wanted in a previous life.

'It's amazing. I love it. It's the best present I think I've ever had. Thanks so much.' I smiled.

He glanced above me and pointed up. 'You're standing under the mistletoe.'

I felt that warm tingling sensation as his eyes settled on my lips, and this time I knew it wasn't the beer. Was he really thinking of kissing me?

I stared into his topaz eyes, trying to read his thoughts. I wanted him to kiss me. I wanted it so badly.

'When are you going to see Kira next?' Richard shouted to Zach from the other side of the room.

Zach turned his head and said, 'Tomorrow. I need to wish her Happy Christmas.'

'Good.' Richard nodded. 'I've got some medical supplies to take to Mumbi Reserve. You can drop them off at the same time.'

When Zach turned back to me my stomach lurched. He had Kira, and I knew the only reason he would ever try to kiss me would be out of pity. That was the last thing I wanted.

I mumbled something about going to check on Asha, so he wouldn't see the disappointment etched on my face, and slipped out of the door, leaving them all to their celebrations. I got Asha out of her enclosure and played with her for a while before lying in the hammock, my thoughts filled with pictures of Zach and Kira kissing that I couldn't get out of my head. Asha lay at my feet, playing with a rubber ball. If it bounced away from her, she'd stalk it, belly skimming the ground, like it might run away. It was amazing how from such an early age she knew to do it instinctively. Then she'd pounce on it and act surprised all over again when it rolled out of her reach and she couldn't chew on it.

The ball rolled off down the steps. She got up to follow it and stopped abruptly, her hackles going up and her ears pricked and alert.

'What's the matter, Asha?' I rolled out of the hammock and walked towards her, hoping Zach hadn't come to check on me. What if he'd seen from my face how much I'd wanted to kiss him? How desperate and sad would that be?

I saw a dark-haired man in a khaki shirt and shorts outside, peering into Asha's enclosure from different angles.

I watched him for a while to see what he was doing before I pressed the flat palm of my hand to Asha's face, which was my sign to get her to stay where she was. I didn't have my hat nearby to try and shield my face, but at that moment, I didn't care. He looked pretty suspicious to me. There was no reason for him to be anywhere near her enclosure.

I walked down the steps. 'I'm sorry, but the guests aren't allowed back here.' I said, hoping he wasn't another reporter sniffing around.

He turned to me with a smile that seemed more smarmy than happy. His eyes briefly widened at the sight of me, but he recovered quickly, the smile never dropping from his face. 'I heard you had a leopard here that you've been training.'

I stared at him. 'Are you staying at the lodge?'

'Yes.' He looked around him. 'My first visit here. Lovely place, this, isn't it?'

'You'll have to go back to the lodge, I'm afraid.' I crossed my arms. We don't allow guests in this part of the reserve.'

'How is the leopard?' He raised a questioning eyebrow.

I didn't answer.

'I've got a client who is crying out for a well-trained leopard for his circus. They're willing to offer you a very substantial sum of money for it.'

My cheeks flushed with anger. 'She will never be sold to a circus, or a zoo,' I spat. 'Now please leave.'

'I think you'd better do as she says.' Zach had appeared behind me, his usually calm voice was edged with anger. 'We have no animals for sale here.'

The man gave me another sickly smile. 'Everything is for sale, if the price is right.'

'I'll escort you back to the lodge.' Zach gave him a look that said he'd better follow him.

I watched them leave and went back to Asha, stroking her in reassurance that everything was OK.

Zach returned a little later with a thunderous look on his face. 'I can't believe the nerve of that guy. He booked into the lodge on the pretence of being a guest, but he was really just some scout for a circus. We've told him to leave.'

I hugged Asha protectively. 'He probably read that newspaper article and found out about her.' I mentally kicked myself for the millionth time. 'It did more harm than good.' I couldn't disguise the slight edge to my voice. If Zach hadn't talked me into doing it, none of the aftermath would've happened. But then he'd thought he was doing the right thing. So did I at the time.

'Are you sure he's going? He gave me the creeps.'

'He's packing up right now and he'll be escorted off the reserve.'

I tried to shake off the uneasy feeling.

Chapter 16

I wiped the sweat off my forehead with the back of my hand and dragged the final long wooden pole to Zach. We'd been helping to build a boma for the two black rhinos who were arriving for the breeding programme, one male called Baruti and one female called Bella. It was all hands on deck to get it finished in time. The result would be two large round structures with four-metre wooden sides so that the animals couldn't see above, and they would be fortified with electric fencing. The rhino would be stressed by the journey from South Africa, and they needed some time in the boma to get them relaxed and happy with their environment before it was safe to release them out into the wild.

'When are they due?' Zach asked Dad as he attached the pole to the frame of the gate.

'Hopefully tomorrow afternoon. The plane carrying them is too big to land at the airstrip in Jito so they'll be flying to Nairobi and travelling down by lorry.' Dad stood back and surveyed the boma. 'The vet on site in South Africa has just told me that when they captured Bella they found out she was pregnant, so that's an unexpected bonus.' He grinned as Jenna arrived carrying a tray of orange juice and sandwiches.

'God, I'm starving.' I grabbed a sandwich and tucked in. 'Thanks, these are yum.'

'Don't talk with your mouth full.' Zach elbowed me gently in the ribs and stole my sandwich.

'Hey!' I swiped a hand at him, but he jumped out of reach, a goofy grin plastered all over his face. 'Get your own.'

'I don't need to now, I've got yours.'

'Don't worry, there's plenty to go around.' Jenna held the tray out to me.

We all sat down under the shade of a nearby tree and tucked in until it was time to get back to work. If we didn't finish the boma before the rhino arrived, we would be really stuck.

The next day everyone was up early. The cool dawn mist floated in the air as Zach and I took Asha for a walk. Even she seemed to know something was going on, and she kept stopping every few metres to sit down, just watching us with a confused look.

'How does she know something's going on?' I asked Zach.

'Animals have an intuition that we don't have anymore. A sixth sense that can't be explained by science. It's an inbuilt survival instinct they've relied on and finely tuned for thousands of years.' He paused to take a photo of her as she stood with her ears pricked up, head cocked to one side, listening to the sounds of the savannah. 'In the tsunami that swept round the coast of the Indian Ocean in 2004, hardly any wild animals were killed. They would've known what was happening long before the waves hit through vibrations and sound, and they fled to higher ground.'

'I read about that,' I said.

'They know and feel things we can't. You hear of animals travelling long distances over terrain they couldn't know, just to get back home.' He shrugged. 'Maybe we used to have it, too, before we learned how to talk and lost the ability. There's evidence that some people can still tune into it, but maybe most of us are too busy paying attention to other noise stimuli to notice.'

We finished our walk and left Asha in the enclosure. There was an excitement and anticipation crackling in the air. If the reserve could successfully breed from these two rhinos, we hoped to increase their numbers and eventually relocate some of their offspring to other protected reserves and try to ensure they didn't become extinct. It would be a long process, and the weight of the challenge lay firmly on Dad's shoulders, but I took Bella's surprise pregnancy as a good sign of things to come.

'We've just had a call,' Dad said to Zach and me with a huge smile. 'They've landed in Nairobi, and everything's going well so far. Bella and Baruti are sedated in their travelling crates, but by the time that wears off, I anticipate they'll be severely pissed off.'

'All the staff, except the poaching patrols, will be here when they arrive in case of any problems. The last thing we need is a couple of angry rhino on the loose,' Zach said.

'Well, let's get some lunch while we're waiting.' Dad slung his arm around my shoulder and we headed towards the kitchen.

Chef grinned at me. 'Hello, Miss Jazz. What have you been cooking up lately?'

'I made risotto last night,' I said proudly.

'It was pretty good, too.' Dad said.

'It was awful.' Zach wrapped his fingers round his throat and mimed having a choking fit.

I slapped him on the arm playfully and narrowed my eyes. 'It can't have been that bad. You soon stuffed it down.'

Chef waved a carrot at me. 'You'll make someone a good wife one day.'

For a moment I stopped in my tracks as his words hit me like a slap on the back. That was so far from reality it was like saying I'd travel to the moon one day.

I took bowls of soup and a plate of bread to the table to get my mind off dwelling on the fact while the rangers and Richard and Jenna filed in.

Richard sat next to Dad and patted him on the shoulder. 'I've waited a long time to start this breeding programme. Thanks to all your hard work, we're on the way.'

Dad smiled proudly, nodding his head. 'This has been a dream of mine for a long time, too. If this works, it will help Kilingi and the rhino.'

I leaned over to Dad and gave him a kiss on the cheek.

'What's that for?' he asked me.

'For being the best Dad in the whole world.' I hugged him.

Two hours later, the rhino trucks were making their way

into the park and a group of us milled around, waiting for them with excitement.

The two trucks carefully came to a stop and three men got out of each vehicle, wearing the familiar bush uniform of khaki shorts and shirts. They introduced themselves to everyone and we all shook hands. There was a vet, who'd been keeping the rhinos sedated just enough so they wouldn't do themselves any damage in the crates, along with men from the Kruger National Park Service who had dealt with the logistics side of things their end, and who Dad and Richard had been in constant communication with over the last few months.

Richard disappeared to drive the heavy lifting equipment that would hoist the holding crates out of the truck and into the boma.

I sat in the tree next to the boma with Zach, and we watched the men attach a hook from the lifting crane to chains around the first crate. Richard pulled a lever and the crate lifted into the air, swinging slightly as it went. Inside the boma, four men stood, holding onto ropes that were positioned on every corner of the crate to pull it steady. Baruti, the rhino inside, watched us all with a watery stare, probably wondering what on earth was happening to him. When the crate was lifted over the boma walls near the entrance, three of the men ran out while the remaining one jumped up on top of the crate and undid the heavy wooden poles holding the door closed. He slid the crate door up, jumped off and ran out the door as the others secured the entrance to the boma with lightning speed.

Slowly, a nose and horn appeared out of the crate and sniffed the air.

Zach glanced at me, and we grinned at each other before turning back to see Baruti stepping out of the crate and taking slow steps into the boma, investigating his new home. Watching this huge, regal creature with its prehistoric body and thick folds of armour-plated skin was just breathtaking. After the elephant, rhinos were the largest land mammal in the world, and yet, even with their armour and their size, their lives were so vulnerable, hanging in the balance because of their horns.

Baruti shuffled forwards and stopped, his legs unsteady from a mixture of the drugs and being cooped up in the crate for a while. He stayed in the same position for about ten minutes, then trotted forwards and sniffed the ground. We'd left fresh grasses and water for him at the furthest end of the boma. Would he be relaxed enough to feed straight away?

No such luck. He wasn't in the least interested in food. He turned around, walking slowly to the side of the crate and stopping a couple of metres before it. Then he dropped his head down slightly, his myopic eyes firmly fixed on the travelling crate, and ran towards it.

There was an audible gasp as he bashed a hole in the side of it, but he wasn't finished. He reversed up, bowed his head, and rammed it again, letting us know in no uncertain terms that he wasn't happy. After a few more goes he seemed satisfied that he'd let us know exactly what he thought, and he wandered calmly to the other side of the boma and sat down with a seemingly satisfied look on his face before he investigated the food and began to eat.

While he was distracted, Richard quickly hoisted the crate back out over the side of the boma.

Now it was time for Bella.

Because the walls of the wooden boma were tightly fixed together, they wouldn't be able to see each other, but they would know by smell that another rhino was nearby. Dad hadn't wanted to put them in the same enclosure in case they attacked each other, but this way they would hopefully be reassured that they weren't stuck in there alone.

Richard, Dad, and the rest of the men repeated the operation with Bella, but as the crate swung over the side of the truck, one of the ropes slipped off, leaving the crate swinging at a wonky angle in the air.

I gripped Zach's hand and squeezed it tightly with worry. 'God, I hope it doesn't crash to the ground. She might get injured.'

Zach kept nervous eyes on the crate, squeezing my hand back.

'We need to do this quick or the crate might fall,' Dad called out as the men on the ground tried to steady it.

Very slowly and steadily, Richard released the crate down onto the ground to avoid it slipping any further. Three men ran back out of the boma as another jumped on top of the crate and slid open the door. As soon as he did, Bella was out and bolting for the other side of the boma. The ranger ran the other way out of the entrance, and the door was quickly secured.

'That's one feisty girl,' Zach said. 'Let's hope she's got as much get up and go in the mating department.'

Rhinos are usually solitary animals, and realising that they both had company, they went to the inner walls of the boma and investigated each other's smells, hopefully drawing some comfort from each other. We sat and watched them settle down for a few hours before dusk fell and the men drove off on the long journey back to South Africa.

The next morning was release day. I woke up with a feeling of immense hope that was also mixed with sadness. If this worked, I prayed that we could help to increase the population and stop them from becoming extinct like the northern white rhinos, a subspecies that hadn't been seen in the wild since 2006, or Africa's western black rhinos that had been poached into extinction. How could we let that happen? If African rhinos were being poached at the rate of more than one a day, it was anyone's guess whether they would still be around for our grandchildren to see. There was a lot riding on this rhino breeding programme, and we wouldn't know how successful it would be for years to come yet, but at least it was a start.

After Dad climbed onto the loading equipment to get a good look at how the rhinos were doing and whether they looked good to go, he glanced down and gave Richard and Zach the thumbs-up to open the boma doors.

In unison, they swung open the heavy wooden doors and then ran up the tree, making sure they were out of horn-ramming distance. Bella realised there was an open path to freedom first and bolted out of the door, her feet kicking up the soil as she went. Baruti's ears flicked for a while before he, too, realised the door was open. He wandered out at a leisurely pace and looked around him for a while before trotting off across the plains into the distance, stopping every now and then to check out his surroundings.

They were free, and hopefully, with the anti-poaching team on the reserve, they'd be safe.

And as we all clapped and cheered and I felt the tears of emotion prick at my eyelids, it suddenly hit me what today was.

I felt a stabbing pain in my chest.

It was the two-year anniversary of the accident and Mum's death, and I hadn't even realised it.

I spoke to her in my head less and less now as I got caught up in Asha and my new life on the reserve, but how could I have forgotten the day she died? That familiar feeling of guilt welled up in me. It felt like I was betraying her memory. I wondered if Dad had planned the release of the rhinos to coincide with today in the hope it would get my mind off things, or whether that's just the way it had worked out.

I felt torn between the knowledge that all this life was going on without her and the need to keep her memory alive. Was it wrong of me to be feeling some happiness again when she would never be able to feel anything?

As the others headed to the bar for a celebratory drink, I slipped away and walked back to see Asha.

If anyone understood what it was like to lose their mum, it was her.

Chapter 17

I stood back and surveyed the birthday cake I'd made for Zach. It was the first cake I'd made using one of Chef's recipes, and I was pretty sure his wouldn't have looked anything like mine. Both of the thick chocolate sponges had risen massively in the middle into big domes. Maybe I'd added too much baking powder.

I grabbed the bowl of whipped cream and lathered it on the top of one of the domes, then added chopped strawberries and placed the other sponge on top, dome side down, and pressed hard. The result was a wobbly looking mess with cream and strawberries oozing out the sides.

I tutted to myself. I wanted it to be so perfect. I was just about to take off the top layer, scrape off the creamy goo, and cut a slice off the dome to make it flatter when Dad walked in.

He took one look at the cake and burst out laughing.

'It's not funny,' I grumbled.

He tried to stop smiling and stifle the laugh. 'Well, I'm sure it tastes nice.' He turned the kettle on to boil. 'Do you want a cake for your birthday, too?'

My birthday was two days after Zach's and I didn't really feel like celebrating without Mum. I'd rather concentrate on Zach's instead to take my mind off it.

'I think I'll have had enough of cakes by the time this huge brick gets eaten.' I frowned at my handiwork.

'There's a woman from the Cheetah Conservation Organisation who's come to visit Kimani for a few days and see how she's getting on.' He poured boiling water over a spoonful of coffee and added some milk. 'I'm taking her out to find Kimani after breakfast, but you should have a chat with her. The CCO has successfully re-wilded ten cheetahs now. She might have some good advice.'

I paused. 'Is she nice?'

'She's very nice.' He quickly downed his coffee as he watched me squash down the cake. 'Well, I'd better be off, I've got a busy day.' He kissed me on the top of the head and left me staring at the cake.

I heard Zach calling me from outside a few minutes later and rushed down the steps.

'Happy Birthday!' I smiled. 'How does it feel to be nineteen?'

He shrugged. 'The same as it felt to be eighteen, I guess.'

'Are you doing anything to celebrate?' I asked, waiting to hear him say he was going out somewhere nice with Kira and getting ready to cringe inside.

'Nah. I'm not that big on birthdays. I'd rather spend the day checking out the animals than in a fancy restaurant somewhere. Not that you'll find any fancy restaurants in Jito.' He shrugged. 'But I think we should celebrate yours.'

'I'm not that much into celebrating, either,' I fibbed. 'When Mum was alive she would always try and make it a special day for me. It just wouldn't be the same celebrating without her here.'

'Well, I was thinking...there's a music festival in Jito on your birthday. Why don't we head over and check it out?'

I sighed. 'I don't want everyone to see me.'

He ignored me and said, 'It will be a good night. It's not like there's much in the way of entertainment round here. I'll pick you up at seven.'

I narrowed my eyes at him. 'Bossy.'

He raised a smug eyebrow, looking quite proud of that.

'Do you want your present?' I asked.

'You got me a present?'

'Well, I made it.' I shrugged. 'It looks a bit crap.'

'Great! I love crap presents.' He chuckled and rubbed his hands together.

'Do you promise not to laugh?' I looked up at him from

beneath my eyelashes.

He made a sign of crossing his heart. 'I'm intrigued now.'

I led him into the kitchen. He took one look at the cake and burst out laughing.

'Hey, you promised!'

'I'm not laughing.' He slapped a hand over his mouth, but I could still see his eyes creasing up at the corners. 'I bet it tastes really nice. Chocolate's my favourite.'

'I know. Do you want to try some before we take Asha out?'

'I don't know if I dare. It might give me food poisoning.' He eyed it suspiciously.

I elbowed him. 'I went to a lot of trouble to make that cake. Do you want some or not? Because if not, I'll just eat the whole lot,' I huffed.

He removed his hand and tried to give me a serious look, but I could see his eyes still dancing with humour. 'I'd love some.'

I cut us both a slice, placed them on a plate, and handed him one.

He took a forkful and chewed slowly, then he put the plate back on the kitchen worktop and grabbed hold of his throat, making choking sounds like it was poisoning him.

I glared at him. 'Ha ha. Very funny.'

He swallowed and burst out laughing. 'I thought so.'

'That joke's getting old now.'

He polished off the rest of the cake. 'Are you going to make Asha one? Surely we should celebrate her first birthday somehow, too.'

'What would I put in it? Oven roasted warthog or barbequed impala?' I scrunched up my nose in disgust.

'How about we try and take her hunting? Her Mum would begin teaching her to catch prey around now.'

It was bad enough having to feed her carcasses, but I'd been dreading the day when I had to try and teach her to kill live prey. 'I don't like the thought of putting live animals in her enclosure to chase. It makes me feel sick. It's like you're just putting it there to be murdered.'

He nodded. 'I know. I don't like it, either, but it has to be done. She's got to learn to stalk and chase them properly before we can get her out in the reserve doing it for real. If she can't hunt in the wild, she'll die. Out here, one animal has to die for another to live. That's the way it's been for thousands of years.'

I knew what he was saying was right, but it didn't make it any better.

I nodded reluctantly.

'We'll start after the festival,' he said. 'Let's take her out for a walk before I keel over from that cake.'

I kept a low profile on my birthday. I didn't want to go to the lodge and see any of the staff. The most important person I wanted to see that day wasn't going to be around, and I just wanted to forget about it. I didn't even want to go to the festival, but I hadn't really been off the reserve in nearly a year, and maybe it *would* be nice to get a change of scenery.

I showered and changed into some three-quarter length brown linen trousers and a black strappy sun top. God knows why, but I even swiped on some pink lip gloss that I'd found in the bottom of my suitcase. Even if my face looked awful, maybe my lips would look nice.

Yeah, right, Jazz. What are you thinking?

I was brushing my hair when I heard the sound of Dad talking to someone on the veranda. I looked at my watch. Zach was early.

I slipped my feet into some flip-flops with sparkling turquoise butterflies on them that Mum had bought me and hadn't seen the light of day since arriving. I headed outside and saw Dad sitting in a chair next to a very regal-looking black woman who had the most shiny, flawless skin I'd ever seen. She had high cheekbones and oval-shaped deep brown eyes. She sat with her back held straight, a soft tilt to her head as she listened to a story Dad was telling her. She must've been in her early forties, and she looked stunning.

'Ah, Jazz, I'd like you to meet Mandisa,' Dad said to me. 'She's the lady I was telling you about from the CCO.'

Without even the flicker of revulsion on seeing my face, she stood up and held out a slim arm towards me. 'Lovely to meet you.' She smiled, revealing perfect white teeth.

Maybe Dad had already warned her about the freak he had for a daughter.

I shook her hand. 'You, too,' I mumbled, eyes downcast.

Dad stood up. 'Well, I'll leave you to chat while I get the wine.' He looked at Mandisa. 'Would you like red or white?'

'White, please.' Her gaze lingered on Dad for a while before she turned her attention back to me. 'You look very pretty. Are you going somewhere nice?'

My eyebrows crinkled up. Pretty? Was she blind?

I flicked my gaze at her to see if she was joking, but all I saw was a kind smile. 'Er...I'm going to the music festival.'

'That should be fun.' She nodded her head towards Asha's enclosure. 'I saw Asha. Your father tells me you're doing an excellent job with her.' She sat back in the chair. 'It's an amazing thing when you get to see them progress back into the wild. The CCO has done a lot of work with orphaned cheetahs, but the problem just keeps getting bigger. Their population has gone from a hundred thousand to around ten thousand. We need to keep all the cheetahs we can out in the wild.'

Dad reappeared with two glasses of white wine and sat down again, handing Mandisa a glass.

As she took it, her long, slender fingers brushed against Dad's. Their eyes met for a brief moment before she sipped it gracefully.

I watched them both for a moment until Zach pulled up in the Land Rover, tooting the horn.

'I've got to go,' I said.

'Have fun,' Dad said. 'I've heard the music is supposed to be pretty good. We might join you later.'

'It was lovely to meet you.' Mandisa gave me a soft smile. 'We should talk more.'

I nodded, an uncomfortable feeling settling over me. Was this woman after my dad?

I was quiet as Zach drove to the festival.

'What's up?' he asked after a ten minute silence.

Everything. It was my birthday and Mum wasn't here. I didn't want to go to a stupid festival where I'd get stared at. And that woman clearly had eyes for my Dad. 'Nothing,' I mumbled.

We heard the bass of the music before we even pulled up to the field on the outskirts of town. Cars were parked everywhere, and it took a while to find somewhere to leave the Land Rover. At least it was pretty dark. Maybe no one would even notice my face.

I took a deep breath and got out, following Zach towards a crowd of people gathered in front of a stage that had been set up for the festival.

A group of men were playing to an African tribal beat, and a woman sang in Swahili, swaying and jiggling her hips in time to the music so well I could've sworn she was double-jointed. We stood at the back, craning our necks over the people as the beat vibrated through us.

'Do you want a beer?' Zach shouted above the music, jerking his head towards a group of stalls selling food and drink.

I nodded, watching the crowd roar when the singer began a new song with a faster tempo. The people danced wildly, smiles on their faces, letting the music overtake them so they became one with it. By the time Zach came back I was tapping my foot. Maybe this was a good idea of Zach's. It was my seventeenth birthday, after all. Was it so bad to go out and try and enjoy myself?

He chinked his bottle against mine. 'Happy Birthday.'

'Thanks.' I took a huge swig of beer and the bubbles rushed to my nose. I coughed as Zach laughed and patted me on the back.

'They're good.' I nodded towards the stage.

'This is just the warm up.'

The band played a few more tracks before a group of children got on stage and started playing what looked like homemade instruments. One of the girls, who couldn't have been more than five, started dancing with expert timing, and the crowd clapped their encouragement.

I swayed my hips and downed the last of my beer before Zach went off to buy us another one. After he'd been gone about ten minutes, I kept glancing at the stall to see where he was but there was a long queue. The man standing next to me caught my eye and stared.

I stopped dancing and turned my head to the stage to block him out. When I looked back for Zach again more people were staring. I bowed my head and looked at the ground, willing Zach to hurry up and come back.

After another few minutes, Zach returned and handed me the drink.

'They're all staring at me,' I whispered to him. 'I want to go.'

He glanced up at the nearby people who were looking at us and whispering to each other, before settling his gaze back on me and shaking his head slightly.

'Jazz, they're not staring at you because of your face. They're staring at you because you're probably the only blonde, white girl they've seen in town for a while.'

But I knew that wasn't the real reason, and it was confirmed a few minutes later when I heard one woman say to her boyfriend, 'I thought they had good doctors in Europe. How could they leave her face like that? There must be more they could do.'

Zach caught my gaze and shook his head slightly, telling me to ignore them.

I opened my mouth to make a 'told-you-so' snappy retort and caught sight of Dad and Mandisa moving through the crowd. My jaw dropped open as my gaze followed them to a spot at the very edge. Dad's hand rested protectively on the small of her back, and they were deep in an animated conversation.

'Stop looking at them if they're staring,' Zach said. 'They'll lose interest soon, anyway.'

I pointed to Dad and Mandisa. 'I'm not looking at them, I'm looking at Dad and that woman getting very cosy with each other.' Too cosy for my liking. Who did she think she was? Mum had only been gone just over two years. How could Dad be taking out another woman?

Dad looked around the crowd and caught my burning gaze. He whispered something to Mandisa and she nodded and looked at us before they made their way round the outskirts of the people towards us.

'I hoped we'd find you here,' Dad shouted over the music.

'They're good, aren't they?' Mandisa smiled and tilted her head towards the band.

I was getting pretty sick of her annoyingly nice smile by then, and I stood there, glaring at Dad, my fists clenching with anger. 'How could you do that?' I asked.

His eyebrows furrowed together in confusion.

'How could you go out with another woman?' I cried, feeling my temperature shoot up. 'How could you betray Mum's memory like that?' I pushed past them and stomped back to the Land Rover.

'Jazz!' Zach chased after me. 'Jazz, wait!'

When he caught up with me I was leaning against the vehicle, arms crossed, a thunderous frown on my face.

'Get in,' he snapped, unlocking the Land Rover.

I got in and buckled up before he drove off. We were silent for a while before he finally said, 'That was a bit immature, wasn't it?'

'Shut up! I wasn't being immature.'

'Oh, and "shut up" is mature, is it?'

'I don't want to talk about it.' I folded my arms and stared out the passenger window.

'Oh, yeah, that's right. If anything gets too tough or complicated you don't want to talk about it. Clam up. Keep silent. Let everything fester away until it becomes a toxic wound. That's you all over,' he snapped back.

I carried on staring out the window, trying to drown him out.

'Why doesn't your Dad deserve some happiness? Don't you think that's a bit selfish?' He paused, his voice calming down a notch. 'From what I've heard about your mum, she was caring and happy and full of life. Do you really think she'd want your dad to be on his own, wallowing in unhappiness for the rest of his life?'

'It's none of your business. Just shut up!'

'No, I won't shut up.' He jerked the Land Rover to a halt and shifted round in his seat.

I could tell he was looking at me, even though I concentrated out the window with narrowed eyes.

'For once you can bloody well listen to me instead of being so stubborn.'

'I'm not stubborn.'

'You're the most stubborn person I've ever met! I'm trying to be a friend and help you.'

Yeah, right. A friend.

'There isn't a textbook on grief, you know, and everyone has to go through it in their own way.'

'How would you know? Your mum and dad are still alive. You don't know anything about grief.'

'I know that if he's ready to move on, then you should let him. It doesn't mean he doesn't still love and miss your mum. It's not like someone can replace her. What's going to happen when you eventually leave home? Do you want him to be on his own forever?' He took a deep breath. 'You can't change anything that's happened in the past, but you can accept it and move on. At some point you have to learn to be happy with what you've got because this is life, Jazz, what you've got right at this moment. You can't go backwards, you can only move forwards.' He paused. 'And if living out here on the reserve teaches you anything, it's that life is fragile. Death can happen in the blink of an eye, and if you don't live right now, all you'll be left with are regrets.' He shifted the Land Rover into gear and drove off in silence.

After he dropped me off, I flopped into bed, going and over and over what Zach had said. Was I being selfish, or was I just trying to protect Mum's memory? It felt like Dad was betraying her. Betraying the love they'd shared. But in the early hours of the morning I came to the conclusion that Zach was right. No one could replace Mum, but deep down I knew that she'd want us both to be happy. She'd want us to live life to the full without her.

Chapter 18

I woke up the next morning feeling embarrassed about having to see Dad. I'd been rude and selfish and unfair to him. I knew he'd only ever tried to do what he thought was best for me, and it was wrong of me to expect that he should never be happy again. Mum wasn't coming back and we both had to learn to deal with it. It didn't mean that I liked seeing him with someone else, but, like Zach said, no one would ever replace her. It just meant that there would be new memories with new people, and hopefully some happiness for both of us along the way. We had to try and make the best of the life we had now. That's all we could do.

I got up and made a coffee, taking it outside to sit on the veranda with my legs tucked underneath me, staring out across the bush.

I heard Dad stirring and fidgeted with the hem of my T-shirt. I would need to do a lot of apologising.

He walked outside wearing a pair of shorts, a steaming mug of coffee in his hand, and eyed me warily. 'Are you going to have another go at me?'

I set my cup down on the floor and jumped up, wrapping my arms round him in a big hug. 'I'm sorry about last night. It's just that it was really horrible seeing you with another woman. It felt like you were betraying Mum.'

He squeezed me back. 'Jazz, I'm never going to forget her. And I'm never going to stop loving her. She'll always be with us, in our hearts, and no one else can take that away.'

I nodded and sniffed. 'I know.'

'But life does go on. It has to. And I know she'd want us to be happy.' He stroked my hair. 'Nothing is going on with Mandisa and me, but I like her. I miss having female company, and for the first time since your mum, I feel like I

- 147 -

deserve some happiness for a change.' He pulled back and tucked his finger under my jaw, turning my face up to his. 'If something does progress, I want to know that you're OK with it.'

I sniffed again. 'I want you to be happy, Dad. I want us both to be happy.'

He smiled and kissed the top of my head. 'Look, I know maybe I should've tried to encourage you to talk about things more after the accident, but you were just so unreachable. You've always kept things inside and it's not good for you. If you ever want to talk about anything, you know I'm here for you, don't you? Talking to someone can help you get over things. It never seems as bad when you've shared a problem.'

I rested my head on his shoulder.

'And I know you've maybe felt abandoned in the past because I spend so much time either talking about animals or being with them, but it's only because they don't have a voice, Jazz. Someone needs to speak up for them and help them when they're ill.'

'I know. Believe me, I understand that now after being here so long.'

He sighed. 'Maybe I could've been a better father, but I'm doing the best I can.'

'Maybe I could've been a better daughter.' I squeezed him tightly. 'I'm going to speak to Mandisa and apologise for how I behaved.'

'She understands why you were upset, but I think she'd like that.' He drew back. 'Look, what do you say we spend some father-daughter time today? I wanted to talk to you about something, anyway. One of the rangers spotted a wild dog with a poacher's snare caught around its neck and I've got to go and check it out. They're an endangered species, and I want to make sure we don't lose a single one on our reserve. Do you want to come along? '

'I'd like that. I'd like that a lot.'

After we changed and collected Dad's medical equipment

from his office, we headed off in the Land Rover to the spot where the wild dog had last been seen. On the way we caught sight of Bella, feeding on some bushes. Dad stopped the Land Rover downwind of her so she wouldn't smell us.

'Looks like she's settling in OK,' Dad whispered.

'She's beautiful. When will her baby be born?'

'The gestation period is between fifteen and sixteen months. The vet from the Kruger National Park did a scan on her when she was sedated and estimated she was about four months pregnant. Her calf will weigh between thirty-five to fifty kilos when it's born and will be able to follow her in the bush after about three days.'

'And how long will the calf stay with her?'

'For about two to three years, until the next calf is born, hopefully. Without poaching in the equation, she could live to anywhere between thirty and fifty years old.'

We watched her for half an hour before driving off.

'My contract with Richard has expired now,' Dad said as he headed alongside the banks of the river. 'I didn't want to renew it without talking to you first.'

The thought of going back to England filled me with dread. For one thing, I couldn't leave Asha now. And then there was Zach...

'I can't believe we've been here a year. Looking back now it seems like it's just flown by.' I turned my face up to the Kenyan sun.

'I want to stay and renew the contract for at least another couple of years.' He glanced at me. 'How do you feel about that?'

'I want to stay.' I grinned. 'I can't imagine being anywhere else now, and Asha needs me still.'

'You don't know how happy it makes me feel to hear that.' He reached out and squeezed my hand. 'You know, your mum loved it out here so much. We only went back to England to look after my father, who was ill at the time, then, of course, you were settled in school and doing so well that we couldn't really come back like we originally planned,' he said wistfully. 'After I'd graduated as a vet and she graduated as a veterinary nurse, it was a toss up between which countries we'd go to so we could get experience of the big game animals. I wanted to go to South Africa, but there was a lot of trouble still going on with apartheid. Your mum wanted to come to Kenya – said she'd always dreamed about living here.' He glanced around the bush. 'We had so many good times in this place. One day we were out on a camping safari in the Masai Mara, just me and your mum sleeping out under the stars. We'd set up an area for washing ourselves and draped a wind break round it for privacy. She was inside the wind break with a bucket of water, having a strip down wash, and an elephant wandered up looking for a drink. It flopped its trunk over the wind break and took a long slurp! Your mum was so excited she ran out naked just to watch it wander off and came face to face with a bunch of people driving around on safari.' He chuckled, his eyes staring off into the distance. 'We laughed about that one for ages. And there was another time when we were at the lodge having dinner with Richard and Jenna when a vervet monkey suddenly appeared in the ceiling above us and urinated on your mum's dinner. As we all scattered from the table, the cheeky blighter came down and stole the food before getting chased out.' He shook his head softly.

It was the first time he'd told me stories like this since Mum had gone, and I begged him to tell me more, listening with rapt attention as he spent the rest of the morning filling me in on some of their adventures while we drove around trying to find the wild dog.

'Kenya is in your blood, I think,' he said. 'You must've got it from your mum. You're a lot more like her than you realise. If she was still here and she'd found Asha, she'd be doing exactly the same thing as you are now – fighting for Asha's freedom. She'd be really happy to know you've finally found yourself in the place where she felt most at home.' He brought the Land Rover to a stop and looked at me.

I tilted my head to Dad's and we touched foreheads. Smiling softly to myself, I realised something. For the first time, I was able to remember her without feeling like there was a knife stuck in my heart.

We sat like that for a while, staring out at the plains, lost in our own thoughts about Mum until I spied what I thought was a pack of wild dogs in the distance. Using the binoculars, I zoomed in for a closer look.

'There.' I pointed. 'Maybe the one with the snare is with them.'

'Let's check it out.' He headed towards the pack and stopped about a hundred metres away.

I passed him the binoculars.

'I see it.' He handed them back and drove closer, then held his hand out again for them. 'It looks like the snare is buried deep in her neck.'

'She keeps trying to scratch at it with her paw,' I said. 'It must be agony for her.'

'I'm going to dart her with anaesthetic and take a look. I'll need to position the vehicle between her and the rest of the pack while I deal with her, and I need you to keep a lookout. If the rest of them come closer, wave your arms around. As a last resort, fire the gun.' He handed me his rifle. 'You ready to do this?'

'Ready.'

Dad loaded up the dart gun and swiftly fired a shot that landed with the feathered tail of the dart sticking out of her rump. A perfect shot.

The dog bolted, and the rest of the pack got spooked and ran towards some dense bushes, but the darted animal couldn't keep up. After a few seconds, she wobbled on her legs and went down.

'We've got to move quickly.' Dad positioned the Land Rover between the bushes and the dog so the pack wouldn't see what was happening and got out with his gear.

The snare had embedded itself deep into the flesh of the wild dog, and I couldn't bear to look at the injury that must've been causing it a lot of pain and distress. I turned my back to Dad, keeping a close eye on the area to make sure the other dogs didn't return and holding the rifle steadily in my hand.

'These snares are vile. When the animal gets caught up in them, it struggles to try and get away, which just makes the wire dig in deeper. It was probably set to catch an antelope, but they're indiscriminate about which victims get trapped in them,' Dad said angrily, trying to cut the wire and peel it away from the skin and muscle.

One of the dogs from the pack poked its head round the bush, closely followed by another one, watching us with trepidation.

'I've removed it all now,' Dad said. 'Just need to clean the wound and give it a long-lasting antibiotic and it should recover eventually.'

One of the dogs crept closer with several others bringing up the rear. They were still about fifty metres away, so I wasn't panicking. Yet.

'They're coming closer,' I said.

'OK, all done. I'm going to give her the antidote, which works very quickly. As soon as I've done it, jump into the Land Rover and we'll get going.' He injected the wild dog. 'Go!' he yelled.

I jumped in, closely followed by Dad, and we watched the dog stagger to its feet, glance around for a few minutes with glassy eyes, then stumble slowly off to the rest of the pack, who greeted her with sniffs and nudges.

'Well, I'd say that was a good morning, wouldn't you? If we'd left her like that she would've died from an infection or septicaemia, not to mention the amount of pain she'd be in,' Dad said on the way back.

As we neared the lodge I saw a Land Rover painted with *Mumbi Game Reserve* on the side. We headed to Dad's office and I caught sight of Zach and the beautiful Kira enjoying a drink at the bar together.

My good morning had just turned sour.

Chapter 19

'I can't do it.' I held my hands over my face while Zach carried a small hare upside down by its feet as it wriggled to get away. 'I can't watch.'

'She has to learn to associate live animals with prey. We'll start her with small ones and see what happens.'

'You'll have to put it in there.'

I heard the door to Asha's enclosure open and close and waited for the sounds of her eating.

'What's happening?' I asked after a few minutes from behind my hands.

'Nothing. The hare is running around and Asha has just run in the opposite direction.'

I slid a hand back and poked out an eye. Asha sat down on her haunches, watching the hare, as if to say, *What are you doing in my enclosure?* Asha looked at me, confused, and then back to the hare.

Slowly, she got to her paws and crept towards it, her body low to the ground, her footsteps silent, eyes focused completely on the hare that hadn't noticed her. When she got to within five metres, the hare looked up and dashed away from her into a bush.

Asha bolted and ran in the opposite direction.

'I think we could be here for some time,' Zach said. 'We need to stop feeding her carcasses now to try and encourage her to catch what we put in the enclosure.'

My stomach churned at the thought as we sat down outside to keep a vigil.

Every now and then the hare would move, which seemed to spark Asha's hunting instinct and she'd stalk it, but as soon as she realised the hare knew where she was, Asha bolted as far away from it as she could.

After two hours, we went inside for a cold drink. When we came back out, Asha was parading the dead hare around in her mouth like a trophy. When she saw us, she sat down to eat, shaking her head and spitting out fur, trying to get at the flesh with her teeth.

'Thank God I missed it,' I said.

Asha suddenly stopped eating and lifted her head up, ears flicking, eyes alert.

'What's the matter?' I asked her. 'Got a bit of fur stuck in your teeth?'

She stood up, tilted her head, and walked to the opposite side of her enclosure, staring out into the distance.

'She can sense something,' I said.

A few minutes later, we heard a rumbling in the distance.

'Is that thunder?' I frowned.

A smile lit up Zach's face. 'No, it's the annual wildebeest migration.' He took hold of my hand and dragged me towards the Land Rover. 'Come on, we have to get to the Masai Mara National Park. You have to see this. Nowhere else in the world is there such an immense migration of animals.'

We jumped in the Land Rover and took off, heading out of Kilingi.

'Over two million wild animals migrate from the Serengeti National Park to the Masai Mara on their search for food and water. In the Serengeti, the short-grass plains will have dried out and they move towards the west. They'll follow the same route every year.'

'How do they know which way to go?'

'Instinct that's etched into their DNA over thousands of years. One of the most amazing sights is the migration trying to cross the Mara River alive. They have to make it past crocodiles and other predators that are lying in wait for them. The Masai Mara has the greatest density of lions in the world, and they'll be ready to pick them off as the herds become panicked or injured in the crush.'

We drove onto the tarmac main road, Zach animatedly telling me more about the migration.

'That sounds horrible. Poor things.' I scrunched up my face.

'It's the ecosystem in action. An endless circle of life and death.'

'How do they stand a chance if there are lots of predators waiting to pick them off?'

'If they stay where they are in the Serengeti they'll die of starvation. They have to migrate to survive, and they have more safety in numbers. You know, newborn wildebeest can run with the herd five minutes after birth and outrun a lion shortly after that.'

As we headed past Mumbi Game Reserve, in the distance the rumbling was getting louder and louder.

Eventually, we arrived at the entrance to the Masai Mara Reserve and found many other vehicles also trying to find a good spot to see the migration. We drove towards the river past plush, velvety looking vegetation. This was what the migration was looking for.

The plains were swarming with a moving sea of wildebeest, zebra, and gazelles. There must've been thousands of them, all running as fast as they could.

We parked the vehicle a safe distance away from the herds, opposite the banks of the river, so as not to get rammed in the process, and stared out at the magnificent sight.

'That is amazing.' I felt the smile on my face stretch from ear to ear. It was such a spectacular sight to see all these animals instinctively following this same path, year after year. The sheer numbers were just out of this world.

'The animals are terrified. They have a fear of the water itself, and they know there are predators waiting to pick them off,' Zach told me. 'But they have to cross that river at any cost.'

I watched, stunned, as hundreds of animals built up along the banks of the river, searching to find an easy place to cross. The noise of the hooves and cries of the animals must've drowned out all other sounds for miles around.

Then they were trying to move away from the river, back in the direction they'd come, but there were too many animals blocking their path and the only way was forward, across the water. We watched for hours, entranced, as they tried to move back and then forth again.

Then finally, one climbed down the banks of the river and waded into the water, swimming for dear life to get to the other side in one piece. This prompted others to copy, and soon there were hundreds of them crossing in a thick wave of animals.

A crocodile, lying in wait, snapped one of the smaller wildebeest into its jaws, dragging it away from the rest in a death roll under the water.

I slapped a hand over my mouth, watching the wildebeest struggling for its life. Excited by the kill, another crocodile picked off a straggling wildebeest on the banks of the river. The poor animal was too busy trying to concentrate on following the herd and didn't notice the predator until it was too late.

As hundreds of animals tried to cross, the banks of the river became so slippery that they were sliding down into the water on top of each other in a frenzy of bodies. Mothers were separated from calves and tried to swim frantically around to find them. Some were successful and were reunited, but others drowned or were picked off by predators.

'It's horrible to see all the ones that die,' I said.

'Thousands of them will die in the migration, but that only represents a small handful of the calves born each year. If this cycle of life and death didn't happen, the wildebeest population would spiral out of control. This sums up exactly what it's like to be in the wild. Every animal out here lives for the moment because once you've survived the drought and the predators and the river,' he pointed to the migration, 'you have to savour every moment left.'

The sight was powerful. Sad, scary, magical, raw, and inspirational all rolled into one. I wafted a hand in front of my face, eyes watering with tears as I was overcome by a multitude of emotions. Every minute spent out in the bush was a unique experience. Some things only happened once in a lifetime. It really had a way of putting things into a new perspective.

'Every time I see it, it still makes me feel so humble. It's just breathtaking.' He glanced at me and wiped a tear from my cheek with the back of his forefinger.

The hairs on the back of my neck rose and I sat there, staring deep into his eyes. He stared back. I'd just witnessed thousands of animals braving their greatest fear to cross the river in their fight for survival. If they could face how scared they felt about their future, and do it anyway, why shouldn't I?

And in a crazy moment Dad's words came into my head that I should talk about things more. Should I tell Zach how I felt?

I opened my mouth to speak but no words came out.

If I told him, it would be the end of our friendship, and I couldn't let that happen. I needed him more than anything. He'd become my best friend. My only friend.

No, Dad was wrong.

I clamped my mouth shut and turned back to watch the migration, letting the moment float away and join an invisible ocean of other moments that we can never get back. Sometimes it was best to let things stay buried deep.

Chapter 20

For the next few months we threw ourselves into teaching Asha to kill prey in her enclosure. When she progressed from killing small prey we introduced her to baby warthogs, gazelles, and antelope. I still couldn't watch her kill them when they didn't have a chance of escaping from her. I knew she'd have to do it for real in the wild, but this still felt unfair. In nature it would be the sick or inexperienced or the young who got picked off by the predators. It was natural selection. I knew it was a necessity if we were going to be able to teach Asha effectively, but it was a conflict I couldn't resolve so I left it up to Zach, living the scene from behind my hands as he told me what was going on.

'I think she's ready to try and hunt in the reserve,' Zach said after a long and detailed monologue about how she'd just killed a small gazelle with a swift bite to the neck.

Its cries still echoed in my ears, and I shivered, even though it was another scorching African day.

'Tomorrow we'll take her out in the Land Rover to a spot where there's some good prey and we'll let her out and see what happens.'

I nodded reluctantly.

'Come on, cheer up. This is a good thing.'

'It's not good for the poor gazelle.' I jerked my head towards the enclosure.

'I told you this wouldn't be easy when you started it, didn't I?'

'Yes, Mr Know-it-all.'

'Hah, you can talk, Miss Stubborn.'

'I'm not stubborn. I'm focused and determined,' I said haughtily.

'Which is just a posh way of saying stubborn.' He grinned. 'Do you want to go for a walk? Asha will be stuffing her face for ages.'

'OK.'

Zach got his rifle out of the Land Rover, slung the strap over his shoulder, and we headed to the soft sandy banks of the river, which was pretty busy with animals. A couple of giraffe lapped up the water, their legs splayed out in an inverted V shape as they bent down. I quickly checked for crocodiles but didn't see their beady eyes poking out above the murky water or the telltale sign of their ripples. A troupe of baboons screeched noisily like a bunch of excited toddlers, playing at the water's edge before spotting us and making a hasty exit.

A group of jackals was out hunting, sniffing around on the rocks by the river's edge on the opposite side until the francolin birds floating on the water grabbed their attention. The jackals flattened their bodies onto the rocks, their mottled beige, grey, and black markings making them melt into perfect camouflage.

We sat down a short distance from the river, and Zach pulled his rifle off his shoulder and set it down on the ground between us.

'Look, there's a genet.' Zach pointed across to the edge of the water that shimmered in the sun. A small, spotted creature that looked about the size of a cat but with a really long tail and a pointed face took a thirst-quenching drink. 'It's part of the mongoose family, but it looks more like a domestic cat, only longer.'

We watched it lap up the water, eyes darting around every now and then, checking for signs of danger.

'A genet turned up at the lodge one day and didn't want to leave,' Zach said. 'It used to come out of a hole in the rafters above the dining room at dinner time, giving the guests hours of evening entertainment. It stayed around for a couple of years and then one day it just vanished. Maybe that's her.'

I could feel my eyes closing as I lay back and relaxed,

listening to his voice.

'And this was–' Zach stopped talking as his radio crackled to life.

'All units, we have a situation at…' Richard spoke, but the reception wasn't very good and his voice broke off with static.

'Damn, we must be slightly out of range.' Zach leaped up and walked a little way from the river. 'Dad, come in, Dad. Can you repeat, please,' he called urgently, his back to me.

More crackling, then the reception became crystal clear. Zach listened intently to the radio as Richard gave the coordinates of his location.

'What's the situation?' Zach asked, but we didn't get to hear the answer. A crashing sound echoed to my left and a hippo charged through the thick bushes, snorting and flapping his ears.

Distracted by the radio call, Zach took a few seconds to register what was going on.

I froze as the hippo charged. There were no trees to climb to get out of the way, and hippos could move pretty fast. If we didn't get away from it, we'd be dead.

As Zach ran towards me, my brain suddenly kicked into gear. I grabbed his rifle from the ground, dislodged the safety catch in record time, and let off a warning shot in the air.

The sound echoed into the bush and the hippo turned tail and bolted back into the reeds as all the other animals scattered from the river in an instant.

I pressed a hand to my chest, trying to get my breath back, the adrenaline pumping through my body. 'Wow. I thought we were going to be dead meat.'

Zach let out a flustered laugh of relief. 'That was quick thinking.'

I exhaled heavily. 'I panicked for a moment and then just instinctively grabbed the rifle.'

'Well, you could've just saved our lives, so I think congratulations are in order.'

But I didn't have time to be proud of myself or think about what could've happened if I hadn't fired that shot because Dad's voice came over the radio.

'Richard, your radio reception's terrible. What's happened to Bella?' The panic in Dad's voice was palpable.

'I don't want to say on air,' Richard said. 'All units just get here now!'

Zach and I ran back to our quarters to pick up his Land Rover. As we jumped in and it lurched forward, an icy feeling of dread racked me to the core.

'This doesn't sound good.' A deep, worried frown settled on Zach's face.

My heartbeat thudded through my ribs and goosebumps covered my body. It had to be something really bad for Richard to call everyone out, and I could only think of one thing that would be bad enough.

We didn't say anything else to each other on the bumpy drive. I don't think either of us wanted to actually put our worry into words. If we didn't speak it, it might not be true.

As we finally approached Richard's location, we saw some vehicles already there. Richard and Dad, along with some of the other rangers and anti-poaching patrols stood looking at the body of a rhino on the ground.

We screeched to a stop next to the others, and I saw Bella, lying on her side, legs crossed as if in a casual sleep, except Bella would never wake up from this nightmare. Half her face was missing, hacked open and reduced to mangled flesh and cartilage. Her horns had been crudely cut off. This majestic, ancient beast whose kind had walked the plains for thousands of years had been cruelly butchered. Blood pooled around her lifeless body, dried rivulets running into the ground like a river. Flies already swarmed over her, fighting for their share of her flesh, and the grotesque stench of death filled the air. Richard's eyes were red-rimmed, and Dad had the same look of despair on his face that he had at Mum's funeral.

I heard a loud scream and realised it was coming from me.

My eyes instantly wet with tears, I couldn't bear to look at the devastating scene in front of me. I threw my head in my hands and tugged at the roots of my hair as the sobs took hold of my body.

'I heard a shot a minute ago,' one of the rangers said. 'The poachers could still be here.'

'That was probably us,' Zach said.

'No, she wasn't shot, she was darted,' Richard said. 'The bastards drugged her and waited until she went down.'

'There's so much blood, she was still alive when they hacked her face off and took her horns. They just left her to die,' Dad said.

No! No, no, no!

I screamed inside, a hot white rage of fury and despair coursing through me.

I cried for the agonising death she must have suffered. The life she'd never have. The calf that would never be born. And all because someone, somewhere decided that greed was worth murdering her for. She had to die because they thought they were entitled to a piece of horn that was made of keratin, exactly the same stuff that was in human hair and fingernails and had no proven medicinal benefit at all. And the greed was like a cancer, chipping away at humanity so all we were left with was death, destruction, and blood money.

Chapter 21

Bella's death affected everyone badly. All the staff at Kilingi walked around with heavy hearts and red-rimmed eyes. The image of her lifeless, mutilated body was burned into my brain, haunting me when I closed my eyes. What kind of a world were we living in? When had humankind become so ruthless and selfish? I was wrong when I'd told Zach he didn't know anything about grief. You couldn't know and see what was happening to these animals out here and not feel it.

Richard called a staff meeting the next day to talk about where Kilingi could go from here.

I squeezed myself in between Dad and Zach, unable to look at anyone, not because of my face this time, but because if I caught the look of devastation mirrored in someone else's eyes I wouldn't be able to control myself.

'You all know by now what happened yesterday to Bella.' Richard stood in the centre of the room and addressed the rangers and anti-poaching patrols. He pinched the bridge of his nose as his eyes watered. 'We cannot let it happen again. As long as these animals are walking around they're in grave danger. And that goes for the elephants, lions, leopards, cheetahs, and many more on the reserve.'

There were solemn nods of agreement.

'I've reported the incident to the police and the Kenyan Wildlife Service, but I don't hold out much hope of catching these people. We need to increase the anti-poaching patrols and start taking some drastic action to protect our animals.'

'Should we remove the rhino horns for their own protection?' one of the rangers asked.

'There's been a lot of talk about that in the past, but there are several flaws with that,' Zach said.

'I agree,' Richard said. 'The rhino would probably be killed by poachers, even if their horns were removed because they'd spend so much time tracking it, they'd kill it just so they didn't waste time tracking it again in the future.'

'Plus, even if you dehorn them, there's still enough horn left under the skin to be worth the poachers killing them anyway,' Dad said. 'And the rhinos need their horns to defend their territory and protect them from predators.'

'There is an extreme idea of injecting the horns with poison so that anyone who consumes them could die,' Zach offered.

'I've already checked out that option legally,' Richard said. 'Even if we advertise the fact that our rhino horns are poisoned, we could still be left wide open for manslaughter charges if someone dies because of it.'

'That's just disgusting.' I shook my head, failing to comprehend the craziness of it. 'If someone eats poached rhino horn, they could sue Kilingi because we poisoned it to protect the animal?'

'It's pretty unbelievable, isn't it?' Richard said. 'But we're living in a world where the litigation culture is getting out of hand.'

'There would also be a possible problem with the poison leaching out into the rhino, too,' Dad said.

'The only other way to keep them safe is by giving them twenty-four hour guards,' I said, looking up and meeting Richard's watery gaze.

'It looks like that's the only solution. From now on, I don't want them walking a step without being watched.' Richard turned his attention to the anti-poaching patrols. 'There's no doubt we're going to have to hire yet more men, but getting hold of well-trained patrols will be difficult. These are dangerous people we're dealing with. If they think there's any chance of being caught, they'll shoot you first and not even bat an eyelid. There have been cases of poachers even using grenades now. Either they'll booby-trap the carcass or they'll use them if they come into confrontation with us. And our men will be out in the bush in the dead of night with the most dangerous animals following the rhinos we have left. We need people with both the courage to handle potential confrontations and the bush skills, and the animals' protection is only as good as the men guarding them. If we could afford helicopter or drone patrols to regularly scour the reserve, that would help, but we don't have the money at the moment.'

'It's becoming more like running an army camp than a game reserve.' Zach shook his head slowly.

'How did they get in?' one of the rangers asked.

'They rammed the electric fencing again. We were working overnight to get it repaired before we lost any more animals.' Richard ran a hand through his hair.

'She was darted with anaesthetic,' Dad said.

'But they're using all sorts of methods now,' Zach said. 'Sometimes they'll lace vegetation or cabbages with poison and put them out for the rhino. They track them until they collapse and take the horn. Or they poison the waterholes they know rhino use and follow the animals until they die. Sometimes they'll even dart them from helicopters, so we need to be extra vigilant for any aircraft flying over the reserve, too.'

'I have a friend who's ex-army,' Richard said. 'I spoke to him last night and let him know the situation. He's going to provide us with some extra men who will be here in a couple of days, but in the meantime, we still have five rhinos left that need twenty-four hour guards. That's ten men to take two twelve hour shifts per day, tracking them at a safe distance.'

It was incredible that Kilingi had to resort to this. It was jungle warfare in the middle of the African plains, but the war was being fought for animal parts, not land or tribal disagreements or religion.

'I'll volunteer,' David, one of the anti-poaching patrols said.

'Me, too,' Mosi, another of the patrolmen said, shaking his head vehemently.

One by one, rangers and the patrols bravely volunteered to protect the rhino, and they were all assigned a shift and a rhino to cover. As the meeting wrapped up, the heavy air filled with loss and devastation permeated my bones.

We shuffled out of the room, and Zach caught up with me. 'Come on, we need something to take our minds off things. Asha's mastered the art of killing prey in the enclosure, so now it's time to step things up. For the next few months we'll be spending all day out in the bush with her, trying to get her to hunt for real.'

Asha was seventeen months old now and maturing into a strong, lean leopardess. She'd even started trying to defend her kills. If I went near her after she'd taken down an animal in the enclosure she dragged it away, either up into one of the trees or to the edge of the enclosure. It was encouraging behaviour. In the wild, she'd have to do the same if she wanted to stop lions, hyenas, or jackals trying to scavenge from her. Increasingly, she didn't want to return home from our walks or outings in the bush, and it was getting more and more difficult to try and coax her back to the enclosure as she wanted to investigate new sounds and smells and sights. I could see the anguish in her face as she was torn between wanting to stay with me and wanting to go off into her new world alone as an adult leopard and do her own thing. Sometimes, when we got back to her enclosure, she'd go off into a corner and sulk for a while. It wouldn't be long before my beautiful little girl was ready to fly the nest, but I couldn't even think about that now. We'd lost enough for one day with Bella. For now, I just had to try and make the most of the time we still had left.

'I've found a spot on the other side of the reserve that I think would be perfect to finally release her,' Zach said. 'It's got enough trees and the river swings into it so she'll have plenty of hiding places and water. If we start taking her there every day, she can get used to it and think of it as her territory. There are no other female leopards on that part of the reserve, so she should be OK there.'

I took her out of the enclosure and she bounded up to me as usual with excitement, nuzzling her head into my legs and wanting me to stroke her until she spotted her football and nudged it towards me to play.

After a few rounds of me and Zach trying to kick it to each other while she darted after us, batting at our legs with a playful smack and trying to tackle us, we gave up, and piled into the Land Rover.

'What do you think?' he asked as I surveyed the area of Asha's prospective new territory.

It was a beautiful part of the reserve. The river gently wound its way along one side, giving her the water she loved to play in so much, and its banks were covered with thick bush and undergrowth that would provide good cover. The area was bursting with woodland and trees for her to sleep in and stash her kills.

I swallowed back the lump in my throat. One day the little leopard who changed my world would be out here on her own. 'It looks perfect.'

'Good.' He jumped out with his video camera and rifle slung over each shoulder. 'Let's walk around and get her used to it. She hasn't been fed for a couple of days so she should be hungry. Hopefully it will allow her hunting instinct to kick in.'

We walked around for half an hour and spotted herds of impala, zebra, and a few waterbuck. Vultures circled in the distance.

'The vultures are interested in something, so there's probably a carcass down there. I think we should avoid it. There could be lions or hyenas on a fresh kill,' Zach said.

We headed off in another direction as Asha sniffed at the ground and scratched at the tree trunks along the way. When we came upon a couple of giraffes, Asha stalked them for a while but got bored when they took no notice of her. Then off to the side, something caught her eye. A warthog.

She froze, every muscle taut against her skin, staring at it snuffling on the ground. She'd killed plenty of warthogs before but always babies. The adults had large tusks that could seriously injure another animal, and this was a pretty big male.

'She's spotted the warthog,' I whispered. 'Maybe we should take her away. I don't want her to get injured on her first day out.'

Zach nodded and we managed to distract her attention by pointing out some zebra ahead of us. She stalked a few of them for a while until they spotted her and stared over. Knowing her cover had been blown, she sat down and licked her front paw nonchalantly, as if to give them the message that she wasn't the least bit interested in them and was only out for a leisurely stroll.

When we came across a large tortoise, things got interesting. As it retracted its head and legs into its body, Asha sniffed around it, pawing at the shell, trying to get it to do something. Since the tortoise wasn't playing, she quickly got bored of that and looked around to see what else was going on.

A couple of ostriches caught her attention as they wandered majestically through the plains. With her body in a low crouched position, she watched them for a while, inching forward under the cover of the bush. She managed to get pretty close, but they spotted her before she was close enough to pounce and they galloped off. Although leopards can run about forty miles an hour, ostriches can top fifty, so unless she concealed herself well enough in the thicker bush to get really close to them before striking, she was pretty much going to be out of luck.

She sat down on the floor and watched them go, the fur around her forehead crinkling up and her tail flicking with annoyance, then she looked back at us, stretched out her front legs and got to her paws.

I stroked her head. 'Don't worry, girl. There's always a next time.'

We sat under the dappled shade of some woodland to eat our lunch of ham sandwiches and water, which Asha looked at hungrily and tried to steal, swatting at them with her huge paws. I jumped up and swung my arm in the air, trying to keep the sandwich out of reach, but she was a big girl by then, and standing on her hind legs she was taller than me. I tapped her on the nose. 'No! You have to get your own lunch.'

She landed back on all fours, swiped me on the side of my knee with one paw and padded off a little way from us, plonking herself down in a huff as she stared at the sandwiches and licked her lips.

Just as we finished eating she sat up, eyes alert, ears twitching, listening to the bush sounds. Her gaze fixed on a group of topi about two hundred metres away, grazing contentedly. One of females was limping and straggled behind the herd.

Asha went into her stalking position while we watched quietly. There were no bushes nearby she could use to cover her, but she crept stealthily towards them, her belly almost skimming the ground, her powerful legs silent as she slunk forward through the grassy cover. If any of the topi looked up for danger she froze. With her perfectly camouflaged fur, she blended into the background and they didn't spot a thing.

She got to within twenty metres and still hadn't been noticed. The limping topi was now further back from the herd, engrossed in feeding.

Then Asha was off in a powerful explosion of speed and grace, and in seconds she'd launched onto the topi, bringing it to the ground. She pinned it down and administered a bite to the neck as the rest of the herd bolted, sounding out warning cries.

The topi's legs writhed in the air for a few minutes, struggling to get away, and I was filled with a mixture of revulsion and pride. But this was the life of a predator, and she'd done exactly what she needed to do.

It wasn't a clean kill, and the cries of the struggling topi filled the air. I pressed my hands over my ears, trying to drown out the sound as Asha lay on the ground, her jaws still clamped around its neck, looking at us. When the topi stopped struggling and she sensed it was dead, she sat up, panting while she tried to get her breath back from the exertion. She'd killed it successfully, but now what would she do?

On the horizon, I saw a group of hyenas appear, attracted by the sounds of the topi.

'Uh oh,' I said. 'She's going to have company.' I watched with trepidation to see how Asha would respond.

Asha hadn't noticed the hyenas yet, and although I wanted to scream out a warning to her, I kept quiet. I was torn between wanting to get her away from them and seeing how she dealt with it. This would be a test she'd come across all too often in the future, and she'd be faced with losing a kill to lions or scavengers like hyenas.

Zach nodded to a nearby tree, indicating for us to climb it so we'd be out of the way of the hyenas if anything happened.

Asha sank her jaws into the soft underbelly to start feeding, oblivious to the hyenas creeping closer.

I chewed on my thumbnail and watched the hyenas get within about fifteen metres of her. She looked up at them, teeth still in the topi, and growled a low rumbling sound.

The hyenas stopped for a second, their beady eyes assessing the situation before they split the pack. Three went round to the back of Asha while four remained in front. Asha turned her head to check out the ones behind and the hyenas at the front moved forward, jaws snapping as they tried to take hold of the topi's legs and drag it away.

Asha lunged forward and snapped back at them, which left the way clear for the hyenas at the back to jump onto the kill and start feeding. Seeing what was happening Asha turned around and growled at them. They scattered and then regrouped as the hyenas at the front advanced. Poor Asha was turning her head back and forth and trying to defend her kill, but there was no hope. The hyenas wouldn't leave her alone, and rather than risk a nasty bite she slunk off and left them to feed with one last look over her shoulder at them.

'Leopards only get to eat about one out of five kills,' Zach said. 'She'll have to learn to be quicker than that to get it up in the trees to safety.'

'She did a good job, though. At least she managed a kill.'

Seeing us, Asha climbed up the tree and draped herself in the branches next to us, staring out at the hyenas forlornly.

'You need to bring it up here, next time, Asha,' I said. 'They won't be able to get it in the trees.'

Every day we repeated the process, driving out to what would be her territory and encouraging her to hunt for herself. Some days she managed a kill, some days she didn't, but I was pleased that she seemed like a natural hunter. She'd remembered that to keep her food away from the scavengers, she needed to stash it in a tree as soon as possible or risk losing it. She had a few near brushes with lions, hyenas, and jackals, but every day there was a new lesson learned.

One day she was lying in a tree, lazily surveying the area with her bird's-eye view when a herd of impala wandered up underneath her, gently nibbling on the shoots below. Silently, Asha got to her paws and leaped onto the back end of one of them. Crumbling under Asha's weight, the impala dropped to the ground, and in a flash Asha's jaws were clamped around its neck as the rest of the herd darted away to safety. A job well done without Asha expending too much energy, and it was a tactic I saw her use time and time again. Her stealth and cunning never ceased to amaze me, often waiting in ambush in the trees for her dinner to come to her.

Gradually, we moved further and further away from her as she investigated her new territory, letting her out of the Land Rover and driving to places where we could watch her with binoculars, hoping she'd get more used to being out in the bush on her own. At first she would watch us driving off and chase after us, but as soon as she knew we weren't going away completely, she seemed to enjoy having more freedom and swaggered through the bush with the arrogance of knowing that she was truly aware of her own power as a predator.

On one occasion she began sniffing around some bushes and flushed out a baby warthog. It shot out, squealing and running for dear life. On hearing its cries, the warthog's mother came charging after it towards Asha. As Asha caught the baby in a chokehold, the mother tried to ram Asha with her tusks, missing her by an inch.

I scrunched up my face with worry, watching Asha leap into the air in an amazing display of agile acrobatics. She just managed to get out of the way of its long tusks before running off with the squealing baby warthog in her mouth. She straddled it and dragged the animal up into the nearest tree. The mother chased close behind, and unfortunately, Asha was in such a hurry to get away that as she climbed the branches, she lost her grip on the animal and it fell back down to the ground with a thud. Surprisingly, it didn't seem to be injured, only dazed, but Asha wasn't giving up her prize that easily and she leaped down after it, even though the mother was trying to shoo it away to safety. As Asha ran after them, the mother warthog turned and faced her, ramming its tusks into her with blind fury.

Asha tried to leap out of the way, but it was too late. A tusk sank into Asha's chest, blood running down her golden coat, and the warthog sprinted away to safety.

A sickening chill crept over me as Asha limped towards us, looking very sorry for herself.

We bent down in front of her and examined the wound. She had a hole about two centimetres in diameter torn through her fur that went right into the muscle, and she was clearly in pain.

'We need to get her back to Dad so he can patch her up,' I said, biting my lower lip, worried that it might've done some damage to the muscle that could impair her future hunting skills.

I stroked her head as she nudged it against me, looking for some sympathy. Reaching underneath her, I ran my fingers along her belly, which she adored. Instantly, she flopped onto her back and stretched out, loving the attention.

Zach called Dad on the radio and we took her back to the enclosure.

'Do you think she'll be OK?' I blurted out to Dad before he'd even had time to examine her properly.

'Give me a chance.' Dad pulled the wound open slightly between his thumb and forefinger, checking to see how deep it was. 'It should be OK, but it will take a while to heal. I'll give her a shot of long-lasting antibiotics and suture the wound, but I'll need to anaesthetise her. She won't be too happy about it.'

Dad performed the operation in his surgery, and we brought her back to the enclosure to recuperate. For a week Asha moped around limping, feeling very sorry for herself as the wound healed.

'At least she learned a valuable lesson,' Zach said. 'She'll know never to put herself in a position so close to those tusks again.'

'Hopefully,' I said.

But what would happen when she was finally released and out in the big reserve alone? I wouldn't always be around to protect her and make sure she was OK. A leopard's life was fraught with danger every day. If she wasn't trying to keep away from lions or hyenas, then she risked possible injury from her prey, infections from wounds or other illnesses, and poachers. Hundreds of things could go wrong. I was doing all I could to try and teach her how to live like a wild leopard, but in the end it was all down to Asha.

Chapter 22

It was Christmas Day again. Where had all the time gone? I was definitely going to make sure I didn't stand anywhere near the mistletoe this year, and I'd finally accepted the fact that Zach and I would never be more than just friends. Surely it was better to have a friend like him than risk it all because he'd never feel the same way about me, wasn't it?

I still missed Mum, of course, I did, but this year it wasn't like a heavy despair crushing my chest anymore. The sharp edges of pain had blurred into a sad acceptance of the truth. Mum wasn't coming back, no matter how much I wished for it. I couldn't change the past, but I could change the future, and my future lay here, in Kenya, the country she loved so much. Now I felt like she was watching over me, proud of what I'd achieved so far with Asha and how much my life had changed since I arrived. I thought back to the day I'd found my beautiful little girl and how depressed I'd been before she came into my life. Without her, who knew what would've happened to me. In my darkest times the thought of suicide had crept into my head. Everything had seemed so hopeless and lost, but Asha gave me a reason to get up in the mornings. She was the one who'd given me the strength and courage to go on. Asha was my see-through leopard. She hadn't seen what everyone else saw when she looked into my face that day. She'd seen through the scars and the pain and anger inside me and saw something that she instinctively felt I could be. I'd jumped into that dark, swampy river but somewhere along the way, the light had pierced through the darkness and I'd kicked my way out of the murkiness towards the surface.

I was sure deep down now that somehow Mum had made

it happen. How else could I have been in the right place at the right time to find Asha? She was sending me a message from beyond the grave that good things can come out of bad. That even if I couldn't heal my facial scars, I could heal my heart and my head by concentrating on doing something meaningful. That I could channel my grief into new possibilities, where I could grow and learn from everything that had happened.

Slowly, I was piecing myself back together, but it wasn't the old Jazz that I was looking for anymore, it was the new Jazz. The girl who saved Zach from a hippo, the girl who fought to train a leopard so she could live her life as nature intended, in the wild; the girl who witnessed the horrifying mutilation of a rhino. The new Jazz was a girl whose heart now lay with the animals. A girl who wanted to try and make a difference to the conservation of wildlife. A girl with a purpose who had hope for the future.

One thing I knew for certain was that I couldn't just sit around and do nothing while the slaughter of these animals was going on. Asha's mum, Bella, Houdini's herd, all the other creatures who were being killed because they had something humans wanted. I had to at least try to do something about it, and I knew that this was the direction Mum had been trying to show me, because everything that had happened since we arrived in her beloved Kenya had led to this point. I'd thought my dreams of being a lawyer and fighting for justice had been smashed into oblivion with the accident, but in fact, they hadn't at all. They'd evolved into something better. I was still determined to fight for justice, but this time it would be for animals, not humans.

I slipped out of the house as dawn broke and slung my rifle over my shoulder. I had something important to do. I picked some wild flowers, taking care to find just the right colours. Holding them to my nose, I inhaled their sweet scent and carried on, walking towards the rocks where I'd found Asha a lifetime ago.

I stood at the base of the rocks, rested the flowers on the

ground, and turned my face up to the sky, feeling a tranquillity radiating through the still morning air deep into my soul.

'Thank you, Mum,' I said into the silence.

I climbed to the top of the rocks and sat there for a while, arms hugging my knees as I looked out across the savannah. A black butterfly with turquoise markings landed next to me on the rock, and I knew it was another sign from Mum. In my heart I knew that she'd forgiven me.

Here, where my journey had begun with Asha, I felt a gentle peace settle over me. I was ending an old chapter in my life and writing a new one, just like Aunt Katrina had told me I could in the beginning.

After an hour, I climbed down and strolled slowly back to the house. Dad sat on the veranda with Zach, drinking coffee. They stood up when they saw me, anxious expressions on their faces.

'Where did you get to?' Dad asked.

I gave them a happy, relaxed smile. 'I had something important to do.' I walked towards him and slipped my arms round his waist. 'Happy Christmas, Dad.'

'Happy Christmas, sweetheart.' He squeezed me back.

I looked at Zach, who picked up a package on the table that was wrapped up.

'Happy Christmas. I've brought a present.' Zach held it out for me.

I stepped out of Dad's arms and took it, unwrapping the package carefully.

It was a radio collar.

'I've always wanted one of these.' I smirked. 'I heard they're wearing them on the catwalk this season.'

Zach laughed. 'It's not for you. From now on we need to swap Asha's collar for a radio collar. She's hunting successfully enough for us to leave her alone in the bush during the day and collect her at night to sleep in the enclosure. It will be a soft release. This will allow us to track her.'

'Well, let's go and try it out before Christmas dinner.' I walked down the stairs towards Asha's enclosure.

Even though I was spending less time in close proximity with her, Asha still responded to me with such love and trust that very few people ever get to experience. I was one of the lucky ones.

I removed her old leather collar and slipped on the new one, which was heavier and more cumbersome. Immediately she sat down and pawed at it, making an annoyed whining sound.

'Don't worry, she'll get used to it,' Zach said when he saw my worried face.

'I'm just an overprotective mother.' I led her out to the Land Rover, and as we drove to her territory, the excitement of the trip seemed to distract her from any discomfort with the collar. She sat, eyes bright with anticipation, watching the animals go by and sniffing the air.

We let her out of the vehicle and drove off into the distance. I watched her with binoculars while Zach filmed her. She leisurely scratched a couple of tree trunks with her claws, marking her territory, and wandered off towards a herd of buffalo. She lay down and watched them for a while and then, deciding they were probably too big for her, made her way down to the river to drink. After satisfying her thirst, she padded away, following an old elephant track etched through some thick grasses and scrubland.

Suddenly, Baruti emerged from the cover, his huge rhino body blocking her path. Asha froze, one paw still in the air as the two eyed each other with surprise before weighing up the other to see who would have right of way. After a few minutes, Baruti must've decided she wasn't worth the effort and retreated back under cover.

Asha swaggered off again, stopping at a large, low-lying bush to sniff around for a while, every muscle taut with excitement. A few minutes later, a large warthog came flying out, narrowly missing Asha's front legs. She chased after it and made the kill with perfect timing and precision, and,

- 177 -

more importantly, she'd wisely learned to avoid the warthog's substantial weapons. Silencing the animal instantly with a bite to the underside of its throat, her strong jaws clamped onto it in a death grip before she dragged it between her front paws effortlessly up into a nearby tree.

'Did you get all that on film?' I turned to Zach, eyes wide with pride.

He grinned. 'All of it.'

'Wasn't she amazing?'

He nodded. 'She did good.'

'My little girl is all grown up.' I sighed with happiness. 'Do we really have to leave her now? Do you think she's ready to be out here on her own?' I frowned.

He nodded firmly. 'She's ready. It would be best to leave while she's distracted with the kill. We'll be back before it gets dark to put her in her enclosure for the night.'

And as we drove off to the lodge, I kept looking at her until she was just a speck in the distance, my throat squeezed tight with betrayal by sneaking off when her back was turned. For the first time, she would be out there without me close by, watching her every move.

As soon as we arrived back at the lodge kitchen, I made Zach fire up the laptop so we could track Asha's movements on her radio collar.

'She hasn't moved,' Zach said. 'She's probably still feeding.'

Satisfied things seemed OK, I helped Jenna and Chef pile up the sumptuous turkey feast and carry it to the table, where a lot of hungry rangers were ready and waiting.

I took a seat between Dad and Zach as Bobo tried to steal a piece of turkey off my plate.

'Hey, that's mine,' I gently scolded and kept my beady eye on her.

Richard stood up with an ice cold beer in his hand. 'Time for a toast, I think. To Kilingi and all the animals in it. Let's hope we have safe and happy times ahead.'

'To Kilingi!' everyone cheered before tucking in.

'You're out of beer,' Richard said to Dad. 'Do you want another?'

He shook his head. 'No, I've got to release that bushbaby tonight so one had better be my limit. It was brought in with an injured leg a few days ago, and I've stitched him up and given him an antibiotic shot, but I don't want to keep him any longer than necessary.'

I looked at Dad. After everything that had happened, he deserved a nice relaxing day with his friends. 'Zach and I can do that for you, if you want to stay here and celebrate Christmas, can't we, Zach?' I elbowed Zach.

Zach nodded. 'No problem.'

'And anyway, I've never seen a bushbaby, so it will be good for me.'

'Well, thanks.' Dad stood up. 'Looks like I'm having another beer, after all!' He walked to the fridge, grabbed one for himself and offered some to the others.

'We can release it on the way to pick Asha up,' I said to Dad.

'Actually, you'll need to do it at night.' Dad sat down at the table. 'Bushbabies are nocturnal creatures with huge eyes that are very sensitive to sunlight, so they forage at night.'

'Well, it's a full moon tonight, which will mean we can still see the release and make sure it goes off OK.' Zach nodded.

'OK, sounds good.' I stared at the mapping system on the laptop that I'd been keeping a close eye on throughout dinner. A red dot was bleeping, indicating that Asha had changed her location. 'Look, she's on the move! I wonder what she's doing,' I said wistfully, popping a piece of roast potato into my mouth.

'Probably working off her Christmas dinner,' Dad said, rubbing his stomach. 'Which is what I'll have to do after this amazing meal.' He raised his beer bottle in the air. 'Another toast. To Chef, for feeding this entire hungry rabble and always smiling.'

We toasted Chef with laughter.

He turned from preparing the dinner for the guests and took a bow of honour with the same toothy grin plastered all over his face.

Slowly, we all went round the table, offering up a toast to someone or something. We toasted the rangers and patrols, the sunshine, beer, whiskey, until it rapidly got more and more stupid and we ended up toasting hedgehogs' spikes, Action Man, bow ties, and pot plants.

I drank the last of my beer, feeling warm and contented. All around me, these people were like a new family. It could be tough living out here on a game reserve in the middle of Kenya, but we all had to rely on each other to help make it work. Mum might not be part of our family in physical terms anymore, but she would've loved to be part of this one, and I knew she was out there somewhere, looking down at us and smiling.

I glanced at Dad and Zach, and their eyes sparkled with happiness.

I felt it, too. Happiness had been creeping up on me for a while, but for the first time I didn't feel guilty about it. Zach was right when he'd said life is fragile, and I realised that the only way to deal with that was to get busy living again. I could've died in that accident, too, but I'd been given a second chance and I had to use it for something good; that's what Mum would've told me. Life wasn't a given, it was a gift.

I sat back in my seat, smiling as I pushed my plate away, too stuffed to move. Glancing at the laptop, I saw Asha's signal wasn't moving. She was stationary somewhere. Maybe up in a tree, surveying her territory. Maybe lying in wait to ambush some unsuspecting prey. I wondered if she was thinking of me, missing me as much as I missed her.

'What do you think she's doing?' I whispered to Zach.

'I don't know. I haven't got X-ray eyes,' he drawled.

'I know, but still, what do you think?' I ignored the sarcasm in his voice.

He was about to say something when all of a sudden a

snake fell out of the rafters above and landed on top of the table, slap bang in the middle of the turkey.

Surprised, I leaped up with shock as everyone else just stared at the snake and started laughing, like it was the most normal thing in the world to have a snake drop in for a spot of Christmas dinner. In Africa, it probably was.

'Get that thing out of my kitchen!' Chef yelled, still smiling as he ran to the table with his hands pressed to his cheeks.

'It's only a brown house snake. It's harmless.' Dad laughed.

'I'll put it in a soup if it stays here, I warn you.' Chef wagged his fingers at everyone as the snake tried to slither off the table.

Grabbing it beneath its head, Richard expertly picked it up and deposited it outside.

'That's nothing.' Jenna chuckled. 'One time we had a huge cobra drop onto one of the guest's tables when they were eating in the dining room. You should've seen their face!'

After all the laughter had died down, Christmas pudding had been eaten, and crackers pulled, I whispered into Zach's ear. 'Shall we go and find Asha now?'

He nodded and we slipped out as the anti-poaching patrols and rangers left to get back to work, leaving Dad, Richard, and Jenna playing a game of Scrabble.

As soon as Asha heard the Land Rover pull up, she ran towards us, her powerful legs taking long strides. She could always differentiate between our Land Rover and the others on the reserve. I jumped out and hugged her close, and she buried her head in my arms. Then she sat back and stared at me for a while, and I couldn't work out if she was trying to say, *Didn't I do well?* or *Why did you go and leave me?*

'Come on, Asha.' I patted the seat of the Land Rover and she jumped in, nuzzling into me as I sat down next to her. 'Happy Christmas, girl,' I whispered into her neck.

As we pulled up to her enclosure, Zach looked at his watch. 'Do you want to drop her off and head back to the lodge? We've got a few hours to kill before we release the bushbaby, and it sounds like Mum and Dad and your dad are still up there, having a good time.

I nodded and jumped out. 'Asha's probably tired out after her exciting day, anyway.'

As if to prove the point, Asha padded slowly behind me into her enclosure and lay down, resting her head on her paws before closing her eyes.

We joined in a raucous game of Scrabble that was still going with Richard, Jenna, and Dad for a couple of hours until it got dark. As they were arguing good-naturedly over the finer points of a two-letter word Dad had just put down, Zach turned to me and said, 'You ready to release the bushbaby?'

I nodded, following him to Dad's office, and he flipped the lights on. There was a cage resting on the floor with a sheet round it.

'Can I have a look at it?' I nodded to the cage.

'Better wait until we're outside in the dark. Don't want to scare him, they're very timid, and the light will hurt his eyes.'

Zach carried the cage to the Land Rover, and he lifted up the corner of the sheet for me to see. A small, furry, cuddly-looking animal with the hugest eyes and ears looked back at me, blinking. I quickly pulled the sheet back and jumped in.

'It's so cute!'

'We had one relocated here about five years ago, and when we released it, it kept coming back to the lodge. It seemed to prefer the company of people over its own species. But it had a bit of a craving for wine. It would hang around the bar, and if the guests weren't paying attention, they'd turn round to find its head in their wine glass.' He chuckled. 'Actually, in Swahili there's a phrase called *kama komba*, which means to act like a bushbaby. The locals use it to describe someone who's been drinking too much.'

'So they're actually sneaky alcoholic party animals.' I raised an eyebrow. 'And they look so sweet and innocent.'

'This one was found near the river on the other side of the reserve, so that's where we're going to release it.'

The sounds of the night filled the air as we drove in companionable silence. That was the thing with Zach, it never felt like I had to chat awkwardly about stuff all the time. The silence never felt uncomfortable.

'This is the spot.' He jumped out and went round to the back of the Land Rover to get the cage.

The raucous sounds of frogs and crickets permeated the night air with their loud chirps and trills and rasps as Zach carried the cage to the bottom of the nearest tree. He set it down, removed the sheet, and undid the latch. The bushbaby's eyes reflected in the moonlight. It blinked at us and turned its head slowly, looking around like it was stunned.

We stood back next to the Land Rover and watched it gain courage before crawling out and climbing up the tree to freedom.

Every time we released an animal that had been treated for illness or injury, I felt so privileged to watch something magical. And although I longed for the day that Asha would be released into her natural world, I was going to miss her like crazy.

I wiped the corner of my eye with a fingertip.

'Are you OK?' Zach said.

'I'm just happy for it.'

'You might see it again if it works out there's wine at the lodge.' He grinned and jumped in the Land Rover.

On the way back we saw the lion pride that had chased me up the tree that night and a couple of hippos that had left the river to feed on the newly sprouted grasses.

Zach gave the hippos a wide berth. After the incident we'd had with the hippo, I never wanted to get too close to one again.

We pulled to a stop outside our quarters, the vehicle lights shining on Asha's enclosure. I knew immediately that something was wrong. The padlock on the door was lying on

the ground, and the door was wide open.
Asha was nowhere to be seen.

Chapter 23

We both sprinted towards the enclosure, my stomach churning with fear. The night air was suddenly still. Eerily still.

Maybe she was hiding in the dark corners. Maybe my eyes were playing tricks on me and I wasn't really seeing what I dreaded was true.

We rushed inside.

'Asha!' I called out into the dark night.

She wasn't there. I spied the half-eaten carcass of a small gazelle and frowned, confused.

'I didn't feed Asha anything tonight. How did that get there?'

Zach's eyes widened with horror. 'I hope it's not what I'm thinking.'

That was when I noticed her radio collar on the ground by her water bowl. It looked like it had been stamped on.

I carried on calling out to her as Zach bent down and picked up the radio collar and the padlock. Then he looked on the ground around the entrance to the enclosure, examining it carefully.

'Asha!' I yelled out, looking around frantically.

I rushed into the house, hoping somehow that she was inside, but there was no sign of her. Maybe Dad had come back from the lodge and brought her into the house for some reason. Yes, that was it. It had to be.

But Dad wasn't there, and neither was Asha.

When I ran back outside Zach was on the radio. 'Yes, she's gone. There are fresh vehicle tracks here. The tyre tracks look like they're from a large vehicle, maybe a truck or van. I can see two unknown male footprints. Her collar's been removed, too.'

Richard's voice sounded strained as it crackled over the radio. 'The poaching patrols are all back out in the reserve now. I'll get in touch with them and ask them to search the area. Follow the vehicle tracks in the Land Rover. Nathan and I are on our way now and we'll catch up.'

'Roger that.' Zach handed me the radio and ran back to the Land Rover. 'Come on. We've got no time to waste.'

He took off and I slammed the door while we were moving.

'Do you think they've killed her?' I shrieked, an icy chill spreading through my veins. I couldn't lose her. Not after she'd come so far.

'I'm not sure. Poachers will normally just kill the animal where it is or remove whatever item they want from it in situ, but the enclosure is near to the house so they wouldn't want to risk someone hearing the shot. The gazelle carcass is bothering me, though. Why feed Asha something unless it was drugged? Which means they may want her alive.' He paused as my heart rate shot up. 'It's too much of a coincidence not to be something to do with that scout from the circus.'

'Oh, no!' I cried.

'I can see the vehicle tracks. Looks like they're headed towards the east side of the reserve. My guess is they'll try and make it into Jito and either cross the border somewhere or fly her out from the airstrip in a private plane. Radio Dad and tell him where their tracks are heading.'

I picked up the radio and relayed what Zach had said.

'We're a few minutes behind you,' Richard shouted over the airwaves.

We bumped along, dust flying in the air, as we followed the vehicle's tracks and I held onto the door handle so hard my knuckles turned white. When we got to the electric fence we could see immediately how they'd got in. There was a massive gap, big enough for a large vehicle to fit through.

'They rammed the fence. Bastards.' Zach sped through the

gap and onto a track that led through thick scrub. Bushes and branches scratched at the side of the Land Rover with a screeching noise, like nails on a blackboard.

I picked up the radio again to update Richard, but he was already trying to contact us. There was a burst of static over the radio before Richard shouted, 'Dammit! We've got a puncture! I'm going to put the spare on as quick as I can and follow you.'

I told him about the fence.

'I'll get onto the patrols and ask them to patch the fence up. The last thing we need is some animals getting out,' Richard said.

We finally emerged through a large dip and bounced onto an animal track. I banged my head against the door in the process as the vehicle jerked around.

'We'll lose their tracks on the tarmac, but we'll head into town and see if anyone's spotted them.' Zach said, manoeuvring onto the road.

The lights of Jito flickered in the distance, creating a ghostly glow. Zach floored the Land Rover at top speed and it groaned in protest. As we reached the edge of town, some kids, who couldn't have been more than five or six, were playing football in the road and Zach had to slam the brakes on to avoid them.

'Have you seen a large van or truck come this way?' he asked urgently.

They all nodded.

One of them pointed further down the road. 'A van.'

'What colour was it?' Zach asked.

'White,' one of them said.

I gave them a pained smile of gratitude and we sped off again.

'Come in, Richard,' I called down the radio.

'Go ahead.'

'They came into town in a white van, we think. We're going to check around and see if we can find it.'

We drove through the main street, eyes scanning the side

roads for any sign of a white van.

Nothing.

Further up the road some men were sitting outside a ramshackle café.

'Has a white van come past?' Zach asked them.

'Yes,' one of them said. 'In a big hurry, too. Nearly knocked me over as I walked across the road.' And he pointed further up the road in the direction the van went.

Within a few minutes we were on the other side of town and there was no sighting of them.

'OK, let's check the airstrip,' Zach said, turning off onto the small, dusty side track, the vehicle's lights reflecting on the trees either side. 'There, I can see the same type of tyre tracks again in the dust.'

I took a shallow breath. Were we too late? Had they already got Asha on a plane to smuggle her out of the country?

I sent up a silent prayer.

Please, Mum, don't let them take her away. I'll do anything you want.

Zach turned the engine off and got on the radio to tell Richard what was happening as my heart raced.

'I'll radio the police and let them know to meet us there,' Richard said anxiously down the radio. 'We've got the spare wheel on and we'll be there soon. Please be careful, these men are probably armed and dangerous.'

'If they're down here, we should dump the Land Rover and approach on foot,' Zach said, his voice echoing in the stillness. 'It might give us the element of surprise.'

Zach grabbed his rifle and we got out of the Land Rover, creeping through the trees towards the airstrip. The moon lit our way as we approached the long path of flattened grass where we'd landed in Kenya so long ago. I could hear the droning whirr of a plane engine start up.

Please let us be in time, I repeated over and over in my head.

Chapter 24

Through the trees we could see one small, unmarked cargo plane parked up at the edge of the airstrip. There was a section in the side of the plane that was open, revealing a doorway for loading. A white van with a metal roller shutter door at the rear had been reversed up to a scissor lift platform, which was already set up level with the van's door so they could transfer their cargo onto it and lift it easily up to the plane. On top of the lift platform there was a large metal cage.

I gasped for breath. They hadn't left yet. But would we be able to save Asha and get out of this alive?

A tall black man emerged from inside of the plane and jumped down onto the scissor lift next to the cage, while a shorter, stockier black man jumped out from behind the steering wheel of the van and hurried round to the roller shutter door at the van's rear.

Zach grabbed my arm and stopped abruptly, his eyes quickly checking out the scene in front of us. He slid his rifle off his shoulder and pointed it through the trees towards the men. 'You stay here,' he whispered.

'No.' I shook my head vehemently. 'I'm not letting them take her.'

Zach glared at me but we didn't have time to argue. Every second was a nail in Asha's coffin.

Zach walked towards them, aiming his gun steadily in front of him at the men as I followed behind. They wouldn't be able to hear us over the noise of the engine, and they were too intent on their task to notice us yet.

The tall man opened the cage door while the stockier man undid the padlock holding the roller shutter closed, releasing the catch on the door, lifting it about five centimetres before he noticed us and stopped suddenly, his eyes registering Zach's rifle pointing at the centre of his chest.

'Stay where you are,' Zach shouted above the noise of the engine, glaring at both of them.

The stocky man's mouth dropped open and he raised his hands in the air. 'OK, OK, don't shoot.'

Zach pointed the rifle at the tall man. 'You, too. Hands up where I can see them.'

The tall man raised his hands in the air, his lips curling into a smile that didn't reach his eyes. 'It's OK, boy, my hands are up, see?'

My pulse roared in my ears as the tension permeated through the night air.

I saw Asha's paw poke through the five centimetre gap at the bottom of the roller shutter doors. 'I want to check on Asha,' I told Zach. 'She might be injured.' I rushed towards the van.

'Wait, Jazz!' Zach said.

At the sound of his tone, I stopped suddenly about three metres in front of the van and the men, whipping my head round to face him.

'You won't shoot us, will you, boy?' the tall man said to Zach. 'Do you even know how to use that thing?'

Zach pointed the gun above the tall man's head and pulled the trigger to fire a warning shot.

The gun jammed and nothing happened.

Zach pulled the trigger again but it didn't fire. His eyes widened with fear.

The tall man's smile became more manic, and in a swift movement he'd pulled a hand gun from the waist of his jeans behind his back and was pointing it straight at my forehead.

'Your gun doesn't work but mine does.' The tall man narrowed his eyes at Zach. 'Put your rifle on the ground and kick it towards me or I'll kill her.'

Zach gave me a worried look and sucked in a breath.

'Do it!' the tall man shouted.

Zach slowly put his rifle on the ground and kicked it in front of him.

I swallowed back a large lump in my throat.

'Get some rope from the plane to tie them up,' the tall man said to his accomplice.

The stocky man climbed up the scissor lift and disappeared into the plane as the tall man jumped off the lift and walked closer to us, his gun still pointing at me. His back was now facing the plane and the van, and I saw Asha's paw wriggling frantically through the gap. The roller shutter door slid up a fraction more.

'Look, you can stop this now,' Zach said to him, his voice pitching higher with anxiety. 'Give us the leopard and you can just get out of here. No harm done.'

The tall man shook his head. 'I don't think you're in a position to negotiate. Do you?' He sneered at us as the stocky man emerged from the plane's doorway and jumped down to the ground with some pieces of rope in his hand.

He looked to his partner for instructions.

The tall man jerked his head at Zach. 'Get him on the ground and tie him up, then do her.'

As my heart pounded erratically in my chest, I prayed that Dad, Richard, and the police would get here soon. Surely by now they must be nearly here, but would it be too late to save us all?

'Get on the ground face down and put your hands behind your back,' the stocky man shouted to Zach.

Zach gave me one last look, as if to say he was sorry, and lay down on his stomach, putting his hands behind his back as instructed. The stocky man knelt on his back and bound his wrists together before doing the same with his ankles.

I saw Asha's paw moving out of the corner of my eye, then her nose poked through the gap under the roller shutter door and she tried to nudge it open with her head. The engine was so loud that the men couldn't hear her. I prayed they wouldn't see her and shoot.

When Zach had been tied up, the stocky man pushed me to

the ground and started tying my wrists together.

'You're hurting me!' I cried, struggling as he tried to pull the rope tight.

The man with the gun walked towards me and slapped me hard across the face. 'Shut up!'

My head jerked to the side with the force of the blow and that's when Asha managed to push the shutter door up with her head. It wasn't much, but it was big enough for her to flatten her body down and slide through the gap.

Asha charged towards the man with the gun and leaped onto his back before he knew what was happening. He fell forwards onto the floor, his gun flying from his hand onto the ground.

Asha dug her claws into his back, growling, her eyes filled with angry determination.

'Argh!' he cried out in pain as Asha sank her teeth into the flesh on his right shoulder. 'Help me!' He writhed underneath her but that just made her more angry.

Zach turned onto his side and struggled to try and stand up but couldn't manage it.

The stocky man looked on in horror. Then he turned around and ran towards the woods.

The tall man's screams filled the air as Asha clamped her jaws onto him tight, her claws holding him down on the ground while he struggled beneath her.

No matter what this man had done, I couldn't let Asha kill him, even if he deserved it.

I ran towards them calling, 'Asha, no. Asha!'

At the sound of my voice she stopped growling and looked at me, her teeth still sunk into his flesh.

'Come on, Asha,' I said, undoing the rope wrapped around my wrists that, luckily, the poacher hadn't managed to secure properly.

Two police cars screeched towards us, their red lights flashing through the night sky and sending shadows dancing on the ground.

I turned to the cars and saw four policemen jump out of

their vehicles and run towards Asha and the tall man, hand guns trained on her.

'Help me!' the tall man's muffled voice called out from the ground. He'd stopped struggling now, realising it made Asha bite down harder every time he moved.

I looked at Asha, her frightened amber eyes reflected the red lights back at the policemen as she bared her teeth, growling, keeping a firm grip on his shoulder.

The tall man moaned in pain. I heard one of the policemen talk into his radio to ask for an ambulance at the scene.

'Please, don't shoot her!' I leaped in front of Asha. 'That's my leopard!' I held my hands out to the policemen, palms up.

The poacher on the ground yelled, 'Shoot it, it's attacking me. Shoot it! It'll kill me! It jumped out of the woods and attacked me.'

'It's a very dangerous animal! Get out of the way!' An older policemen had his handgun pointing towards me, waving with his other hand for me to move.

But there was no way I was moving. Adrenaline coursing through my veins had obliterated all rational thought. All I could think about was saving Asha from a firing squad.

'Don't shoot her!' I cried. 'She's mine. She won't hurt anyone. This man's a poacher!'

'I'm from the Kilingi Game Reserve,' Zach said to them breathlessly. 'That's our leopard. She was stolen from our reserve tonight and this man is a poacher.' He jerked his head towards the trees. 'Another one ran off that way.'

The tall man on the ground moaned again. 'Shoot it! Its teeth are in me. Kill it! These kids are lying. I'm an airline pilot and the leopard ran out of the woods and attacked me. Kill it!'

'We can capture her, there's no need to shoot her,' I said breathlessly to the policemen whose guns were now aimed at me. 'He's not a pilot, he's a poacher.'

'Look, you stupid girl, it's already attacked someone!' the older policeman shouted. 'We need to shoot it now. Move out of the way so I can kill it before it attacks you.'

'No!' I yelled. 'Put the guns down!' I turned around to face Asha and my heart squeezed tight as I saw how distressed and agitated she was. I put my palm to her face to try and calm her down. 'Come on, Asha, let go.' I carried on talking to her in a low voice.

Zach said to the police from his position on the floor, 'She's not dangerous, honestly. She only attacked that man trying to save us. If she hadn't done that they probably would've shot us and left us for dead.'

Slowly, Asha released her grip on the man and her nervous eyes looked deep into mine as she panted hard. She trusted me and I couldn't let her down. Those men probably would've shot us and not thought twice about it, and Asha had saved our lives. If they were going to shoot her, they'd have to shoot through me first.

'It's OK, girl. It's all right,' I whispered and grabbed her collar, feeling the muscles in her neck taut with fear.

I heard a Land Rover speed down the track to the airstrip and turned my head to see Dad and Richard pulling to a stop and jumping out. Dad's eyes widened with horror as he registered the situation.

'Sergeant Abasi,' Richard barked to the older policeman. 'This is a leopard that was stolen from Kilingi. She's not dangerous. Don't shoot her.'

I gnawed on my lip, heart racing. If Richard knew the policeman, maybe he would listen to him.

The poacher groaned in pain and then he slipped into unconsciousness.

'Sergeant, that's my daughter out there!' Dad cried. 'Please, don't shoot.' Dad looked at me, his forehead crinkled in a worried frown. 'Are you OK, Jazz?'

'I'm OK.' I nodded, feeling Asha's head and neck straining against the collar as I stared at the police. 'I need to protect Asha. I'm not moving.'

'Zach, are you hurt?' Richard shouted to him.

'No, I just need untying.'

Richard hurried towards Zach and pulled a pocket knife out of his shorts, cutting the ropes binding his wrists and ankles.

The sergeant looked at Richard. 'The leopard already attacked this man.' He jerked his head towards the mauled man.

'But he's a poacher!' I cried, feeling tears pricking my eyes. 'She only attacked him to save us from being shot.' I sucked in a breath and waited to see what Asha's fate would be. Had we managed to save her from poachers only so she'd be shot by the police?

Sergeant Abasi was silent for a moment, thinking. He looked at me, standing in front of Asha, before he turned back to Richard. 'Can you capture it, Richard?' The sergeant's dark eyes clouded with worry.

Richard nodded. 'Yes, but we need you to lower your guns and move back. It's agitating her.'

Sergeant Abasi turned back to me, quickly appraising the situation.

Zach walked past the armed policemen and stood next to me in front of Asha, trying to shield her from them.

'Get your men to back away slowly and lower their guns.' Richard stepped towards the policemen.

The policemen looked worriedly at Sergeant Abasi for instructions.

'I trust your judgement, Richard,' the sergeant said, then nodded at his men. 'Do as he says.'

Slowly they lowered their guns, backing away. I turned around to Asha and bent down in front of her, whispering reassuring words in her ear.

'It will be OK, Asha. Don't worry. Shhhhh.'

'Bring the Land Rover up to Asha,' Richard said to Dad.

Dad reversed the Land Rover next to us.

'Come on, Asha.' I tugged her collar, encouraging her to move, but she was so scared she'd frozen. 'It's OK. Come on, girl. You're OK.'

After a few minutes of coaxing, she allowed me to lead her

to the Land Rover and she leaped up into the passenger seat. I climbed in after her as she nuzzled her head into my armpit. It wasn't until I sank down next to her that I realised I was shaking uncontrollably.

The policemen swarmed around the unconscious poacher, guns trained on him.

'The other man you want ran off in that direction.' Zach pointed towards the trees and gave them a description.

Sergeant Abasi nodded. 'Take the leopard back to the reserve. I don't want any more trouble with her. We'll come and question you after we search for the other man.'

Zach got behind the steering wheel and we drove away, passing an ambulance heading towards the airstrip.

When we arrived back at our quarters, Asha was very subdued and wouldn't leave my side. I sat quietly in the corner of the lounge with her. She rested her head in my lap and I stroked her soothingly until Richard and Dad arrived back.

At the sound of their Land Rover arriving, Asha buried herself against me. She was probably terrified that someone had come to take her away again.

'We got the other poacher,' Richard said proudly as he walked into the lounge, closely followed by Dad. 'Luckily, here we have the support of the local police and Sergeant Abasi is a good guy, otherwise it could've turned out very differently.'

'How is that man?' I asked. 'Will he survive?'

'He lost a lot of blood and he's got some nasty bite marks,' Dad said. 'But it looks like he'll be OK.'

I couldn't work out whether I was glad or not.

'They admitted everything. They were working for that circus scout,' Richard said. 'They told the police they'd fed Asha drugged meat and then loaded her in the back of the van when she became unconscious. They were going to transfer her into the cage and load her on the plane, but luckily for us, she hadn't eaten enough of it to knock her out completely and she woke up, otherwise she wouldn't have managed to escape out of the van.'

That's my girl. My brave and clever girl.

I dared myself to breathe a sigh of relief, but how long would it be before someone else wanted to take her?

'We're going to need to increase the anti-poaching patrols yet again,' Dad said.

'I agree,' Zach said. 'It's nearly time for Asha to be released out into the reserve on her own, but she's a sitting target in that enclosure.'

'I'll see if we can borrow a few from Mumbi Game Reserve tomorrow until we can hire more people,' Richard said, wearily rubbing his forehead. 'I'll make sure she has a twenty-four hour guard.'

But would it be enough to ensure the safety of Asha and all the animals here? Would it ever be enough?

Chapter 25

It took a while before Asha finally settled down after she'd been stolen. She didn't want to leave my side for weeks, and it always tugged at my heart when I had to leave her in the enclosure, but if she was going to be successfully re-wilded, we needed to try and reduce the amount of time we spent with her so she'd get to being on her own. At least now she had her own guard, called Mosi, whenever she wasn't with me, so I knew she was safe, and I hoped that she'd learned a lesson that night to be afraid of humans that she'd remember for her own protection.

Over the next few months we left Asha for longer and longer periods during the daytime to explore her territory. Mosi would track her on foot at a distance, and she wore her new radio collar so we could track her from the lodge on Zach's laptop. Mosi reported how she managed to successfully kill small zebra, antelope, gazelles, lizards, and every time she brought down prey, Zach and I would cheer. When her hunting wasn't successful, or if she lost a kill to other predators, we'd shake our heads and feel disappointed for her, but one thing was certain: she had honed her hunting skills sufficiently to live a successful life, and was now marking her scent on trees and bushes in her territory as she reached sexual maturity.

My little girl had finally come of age, and it was time to let her go. We would have to try and cut off all contact with her and let her live out on the reserve permanently.

The night before her release was due to happen, I couldn't sleep. My moods swung from sadness to immense happiness. To all intents and purposes I'd been her mother for almost two years, and if she loved me like a mother, then

I loved her more. We'd been through so much together, and I wondered if she'd miss me as much as I would her. Yes, I knew I'd still see her as often as I liked on the reserve, but in the wild, when their mothers left them to fend for themselves, did the cubs miss them? With any luck, she'd be a proud mother of her own soon, bringing up the next generation of leopards at Kilingi.

But then what? I wouldn't be there to protect her anymore. What if something happened to her? I couldn't stand the thought of her being cruelly taken away. I couldn't believe that I'd actually succeeded in re-wilding her, either. All those months ago when I'd found her starving to death and scared out of her mind, I never knew she would take me on such an incredible journey. We'd both come a long way since then, and this was her time. It wasn't the end, only the beginning. She had her own journey to go on now.

I crept into Asha's enclosure at first light and shut the door behind me. Zach was right, animals do have a sixth, or even seventh sense, and somehow she knew that this would be our last time together, because instead of trying to play with me, she just sat quietly next to me, resting her huge paw protectively on my leg and staring up at me like she could read my mind and felt exactly the same way.

'Are you ready to go?' Zach found me a few hours later.

I wiped the tears away from my cheeks and nodded. 'Come on, Asha.' My voice cracked on her name.

As we all piled into the Land Rover, Asha looked at me, instead of excitedly looking out of the window like she normally did. I held her gaze and spoke silently to her in my head.

You'll be fine, Asha. You're going to live an amazing and happy life. I love you, girl. I'm going to miss you so much. Please stay safe.

Zach and I didn't speak on the journey, and as we pulled up in Asha's territory, I just sat for a few minutes, staring out at the bush but not really seeing anything around me.

Finally, I took a huge sniff, wiped away more tears, and

opened the door.

Zach got out and focused the camera on us.

'Come on, Asha,' I said.

She jumped down and sat, staring up at me. I knelt in front of her, placing both hands on her cheeks and staring deep into her eyes. 'Make sure you take care of yourself, do you hear?' I kissed her gently on the forehead and stood up, pointing off in the distance. 'This is all yours now. Live and be happy.'

Her gaze followed where I was pointing before looking back at me, her amber eyes warm with love. Then, uncertainly, she took a few steps away and stared into the distance. I watched her as she stopped, seeming torn between whether to go or stay.

'Go on, Asha,' I croaked out. 'You deserve this.'

She came back to me, rubbed her head against my legs one final time before she slowly walked into the distance. As I got back into the Land Rover, I couldn't control myself anymore and succumbed to the sobs that shook my whole body.

Zach turned off the camera and got behind the steering wheel. He put his arm around me, pulling me towards him until my head rested on his shoulder. 'You've done an amazing job, Jazz. She's ready to go.'

I nodded through a loud sniff. 'I know, but it doesn't make it feel any better.'

'Something truly special has just happened. Every time you think about her, remember that.' He held me for a long time, rubbing my back until my sobs had subsided before we finally drove off, catching sight of Mosi in the distance.

I looked out of the window at Asha's silhouette retreating to the edge of her territory. She stopped, tilted her chin up and opened her mouth slightly, looking like a regal leopard queen.

I wanted to get out and call her. Run to her and throw my arms around her neck and let her nuzzle into me. Feel her soft fur and whiskers underneath my fingertips. I wanted it

- 200 -

so much it nearly broke my heart in two, but I had to let her be a proper wild animal.

Goodbye, my amazing leopardess.

For the next few days I moped around. Zach was busy editing the documentary to send to National Geographic and Asha was busy getting used to a life of freedom. Without both of them, I suddenly felt lost. I monitored Asha's movements on the laptop practically every minute of the day, and lay awake at night, tossing and turning beneath the sheets, wondering what she was doing. Did she think I'd just abandoned her? I couldn't bear it if she did.

On the second day of not seeing her, I didn't know what to do with myself. I picked up a cookbook and flicked through the pages but couldn't take anything in. I wandered aimlessly round the house, knowing I had to try to keep away from her, to let her settle in. I stared at the photo of us that Zach had given me that Christmas. I helped Chef in the kitchen but ended up cutting myself as I chopped vegetables because I was so distracted. The days dragged on forever, and I tried desperately to ignore the raw pain inside. Asha was my drug and I needed a fix badly. The sense of completeness and contentment I had when I was around her was overwhelming, and now there was a huge gap in my life. My thoughts bounced around in a turmoil of worry and anxiety.

On the third day, I woke up early to turn on the laptop and check her movements from the radio collar but there was no signal. I pressed various buttons, closed down the programme and reopened it, but it was still the same. There was no trace of her.

A force like a boxer's punch hit me straight in the solar plexus. It could only mean one of two things. Either the collar had stopped working or something had happened to her. Visions of her being kidnapped again or killed flew into my mind.

I hurriedly pulled on my clothes and jumped in the Land

Rover that I now used after Zach had finally taught me to drive. I headed up to the lodge to get Zach, screeching to a stop outside, calling out his name as I ran through the empty reception, but it was still too early for anyone to be around.

Running through, I made my way to his quarters, a similar structure to the guest rooms but larger, with a kitchen and dining room. Banging on the door, I breathlessly prayed that she was OK and that nothing had happened to my little girl.

'Zach!' I cried as I carried on banging. 'Come quick!'

He was pulling on a T-shirt over his shorts when he opened the door with sleepy eyes. 'What's the matter?' He frowned when he saw the state of me.

'It's Asha. There's no signal from the collar. We've got to go and see if she's OK.'

'Did you radio Mosi?' he asked.

I slapped a hand to my forehead. 'No, I was so worried, I didn't even think of that.'

Wasting no time, Zach got on the radio and said, 'Mosi, come in, Mosi.'

I gnawed on my lower lip and waited for a reply.

'Mosi,' Zach repeated. 'Come in, Mosi.'

No response.

'All units, does anyone know where Mosi is?' Zach called over the radio.

One of the rangers said, 'It was his day off yesterday. He's due back this morning.'

'Who was tracking Asha?' Zach's urgent voice said.

One by one they said they didn't know.

'Shit! How could this happen?' Zach muttered. 'We need to double check the guards' rotas from now on. The animals' safety is only as good as the guards looking out for them. Come on.' He rushed out the door and we ran to the Land Rover.

'I'll drive.' He held his hands out for the keys.

I obliged, since my hands were shaking so much there was no telling what might happen.

'Where did you last see a signal?'

'Last night when I checked the laptop before I went to bed she was in the northern quarter of her territory along the river bank.'

Please let her be OK. Please let her be OK. I repeated it over and over in my head as we drove.

When we got to the area where I'd last seen her signal, we slowed down, driving around the bushes and trees, eyes scanning frantically in all directions.

There was no sign of her.

'Asha!' I called out. 'Asha!'

Nothing.

I bit my lip, waiting for any sighting of her.

'Maybe she headed off elsewhere in the night. We need to drive around,' Zach said.

We drove and searched, an overwhelming fear twisting a knife inside me. The blood pulsed loudly in my ears, and palpitations banged out a tribal beat in my chest.

We had to stop to let a line of wildebeest trundle leisurely across the road, their hooves kicking up a trail of dust. I willed them to hurry up, but they were on Africa time and going at their own pace.

'Come on!' I cried, jumping up and down in my seat. 'Hurry up!'

Eventually, after what seemed like two hours, but was probably only fifteen minutes, we managed to drive on.

'She must be here somewhere,' I pleaded, more to myself than Zach. 'She's got to be.' I swivelled round in my seat, trying to get a three hundred and sixty degree angle.

'Surely she'd hear the Land Rover and know it was us if she was here,' Zach said.

'Asha! Asha, come on, girl.'

'There!' Zach pointed to a movement in a tree in the distance. 'I can see something.' He pulled out his binoculars.

I cupped my hands round my lips and screamed for dear life as the panic rose in my throat. 'Asha!'

Slowly, I saw her emerge. She jumped down from the lower branches and ran towards us.

I leaped out of the Land Rover and sprinted to meet her, tears of joy streaming down my face. She was OK. She was alive!

I held out my arms and she bounded into them, knocking me to the floor. Thinking this was a big game, she swatted me with her paw and sat on top of me.

Through my tears, I laughed with relief so hard my stomach hurt, and I buried my head in her neck. 'You're OK, girl. I thought I'd lost you.'

She sat up and licked the side of my face as I rolled over and sat up, hugging her towards me. 'Don't ever do that to me again!' I stared into her eyes, and she just yawned in response, probably wondering what all the fuss was about.

'Her collar's still on, so maybe there's a problem with it,' Zach said, getting out of the Land Rover. 'Take it off and let me check it.'

I undid the collar and handed it to him as she nudged me to stand up and play. She walked round me in a circle, looking up at me with a shifty gaze, then she lifted up on her hind legs and threw her huge paws on my shoulders, pushing me back down to the ground, where she decided to sit on me again, flicking her tail.

'I think she's telling me off for leaving her.' I chuckled.

Zach examined the collar. 'I think the battery's died.' He strode to the Land Rover. 'There should be some more in here.' I heard him opening the glovebox as I stroked Asha behind the ear.

The alarm call of some antelopes rang in the air and Asha sat up, instantly alert, ears flicking, leaning her powerful body against me. There was something different in her eyes now. A change that spoke of new experiences that I would never share with her. A loss of the dependant, innocent leopard she'd been. My little baby was all grown up.

'You can't go yet. We need to fix your collar.' I held onto her tightly, but I could feel her muscles straining under my touch. She wanted to go.

'Here.' Zach handed me the collar and held up the tracking

device in his other hand, checking the signal. 'It's working now.'

I quickly slipped it round her neck as the call of the antelope became more panicky in the background. As soon as I'd finished doing up her collar, Asha was off, padding away purposefully out of my life and into hers. I watched her disappear into the distance wishing with everything I had that I could walk with her, side by side, like I'd done since she was a cub. We tracked her until another guard took over, and when we drove back to the lodge I felt a mixture of both triumph and worry. I missed her like crazy, but she was healthy, happy, and enjoying the life she was supposed to have.

I decided there and then that I would still drive out to see her every couple of days. I wouldn't approach her, but if she came to me, then it was a different story. A few stolen moments with her in the bush wasn't the same as being with her all the time, but it was all I could hope for now. If Zach could have his elephant love, I could have my leopard love.

In the following weeks, as Zach was busy with the documentary and I was obsessing about Asha and trying to fill the void she'd left, Dad tried to take my mind off things by taking me out in the bush when he had to treat any injured animals. It helped a bit, but I still had a lot of time think.

This had all started with Asha, but now it was about so much more. I still couldn't get the savage picture of Bella out of my head, and I couldn't stand the thought of what happened to her happening to another creature. Animals were being killed for profit in Africa every day, and the world either didn't know or didn't care. How many elephants, rhinos, leopards, lions, cheetahs were dying? How many other animals?

I had to do something, but in order to get things to change, you had to make people aware of it. You had to make people care enough. Extinction is forever. No going back.

The question was, what could I do to help them?

Chapter 26

'I've finished editing the documentary,' Zach said as we sat drinking an early morning cup of coffee on the veranda.

'Wow, you've finished it?' I smiled for the first time all week. 'I bet Asha looks brilliant on film, doesn't she?'

'It's amazing. Even though I say so myself.' He smiled proudly. 'I think you're going to love it. But first I want you to meet someone.' He finished off the last of his coffee and set it down on the table, rising to his feet.

'Who?' I asked.

'You'll see.' He smiled, turned on his heels, and strode down the steps.

I narrowed my eyes at his retreating form and refused to get up. I wasn't really in the mood for meeting strangers.

'Aren't you coming?' his voice called from down by the Land Rover.

'You go,' I said. 'Maybe I'll take a drive out to see Asha.'

He bounded back up the steps. 'You're not supposed to be following her around all the time. How's she going to learn to be a proper wild leopard if you go and see her every five minutes? Come on, this will cheer you up, and you're going to want to meet her.'

'Who?'

'I'll tell you on the way.' He grabbed my hand and pulled me to my feet, pushing me along the veranda and down the steps.

We got into the Land Rover and I slumped in the seat, forehead scrunched up in a frown. 'Stop mucking about. Who are we going to see?'

'Kira.' He glanced at me, his eyes dancing with excitement.

A frown furrowed on my forehead.

Kira? Why the hell would I want to meet your girlfriend when I already feel crappy enough about missing Asha?

'Maybe you should go on your own,' I snapped. 'You might want some privacy.'

He threw his head back and roared with laughter.

What's so funny about that?

I glared at him out of the corner of my eye and gave him abrupt one-word answers as he tried to talk to me.

We drove out of Kilingi and off onto the dirt track that led to the tarmac road, then turned left towards Mumbi Game Reserve.

Zach kept glancing over and smiling.

Oh, God, maybe he's going to tell me they're engaged, or something. And what happens if they get married? Zach will never leave Kilingi. That means she'll move in there, and I'll have to see them all over each other every day!

My stomach turned at the thought.

'You're very quiet. What's up?' Zach asked, turning into Mumbi.

'Nothing,' I mumbled.

'Look, I know you've been sad about Asha, but—'

'Whatever,' I cut him off, staring out of the window.

I heard him exhale a soft sigh and ignored him as we drove up towards the main lodge, which was as grand as Kilingi, and then took a dirt track off to the right.

'Aren't we stopping here?' I snapped.

Surely Kira would be waiting for him at the lodge, wouldn't she? Maybe she'd be getting the champagne ready in the bar for a nice toast to the happy couple. Well, if she did I'd probably choke on it.

He gave me an odd look. 'She's out in the bush.'

Well, good for her! Where else would I expect the future wife of Zach to be? Out in the bush so you can spend lots of time together with your big herd of animals.

'Oh,' I said with disinterest.

We bumped along through bush and trees and tracks that

were pretty similar to Kilingi, then finally pulled up under the shade of a large acacia tree. He switched off the engine, pulled out a pair of binoculars and looked out towards a pride of lions relaxing on some rocks about eighty metres away. There were eleven females with six cubs of varying ages and sizes. The cubs ran around playing with each other or trying to annoy their parents by chewing on their tails or biting their faces.

He handed me the binoculars. 'She's the third one from the right with the two small cubs.'

I took the binoculars and stared at him. 'I thought we were going to see Kira, not lions.'

He jerked his chin towards the pride and pointed. 'That *is* Kira.'

My mouth hung open. 'Kira's a lion?'

He frowned. 'Well, who did you think she was?'

A smile curved onto my lips. 'I thought she was your girlfriend. I thought she was the daughter of the reserve owner. The one I saw you with at the party a couple of years ago at Kilingi.'

His frown got bigger. 'You didn't go to the party.'

'I did, but no one saw me.'

'Why did you think that was Kira?'

'Because you kept saying you were going to see her all the time, and I just assumed that it was Miss Gorgeous Big Eyes who was getting very cosy with you that night.' The vision of them laughing conspiratorially came into my mind, her touching his shoulder, leaning in to whisper in his ear, and him sliding his hand around her waist.

He roared with laughter again.

'What's so funny?' It was my turn to frown.

He shook his head. 'That's Callie. And we've known each other since we were kids. She's just a good friend.'

She was a bit too touchy feely to be a friend. How can she be just a friend when she was all over him?

But then, hadn't Zach been kind to me in the last few years? Hadn't he touched me when he was comforting me?

Hadn't he just been a 'good friend' to me?

'Callie's got a boyfriend at university, anyway. She can't wait to get her degree in business management and get out of Africa to go to America or England,' he said. 'I mean, most girls want wining and dining, and I couldn't offer them any of that. It's not like there are many girls who would want to put up with a guy like me who's obsessed about animals all the time, while they're stuck out in the wilds of Africa, is it?'

But I would, Zach. Oh, God, I would.

I grabbed the binoculars and put them to my face so he wouldn't have to see the flush of relief and embarrassment creeping up my cheeks.

I watched Kira as one of her cubs climbed all over her while she lazily licked the other one's face. She was a beautiful lioness – muscular with a shiny coat that was slightly darker than the others.

'Kira was an orphan, too, like Asha,' Zach said.

'What?'

He nodded. 'Her mother was shot by a hunter in the Masai Mara Reserve. He thought it would be fun to have a stuffed lion as a trophy. Lionesses go off away from the pride when they have cubs. After a few weeks, they introduce them back to the pride. It helps with bonding, but it can leave the lionesses vulnerable. Kira's mum kept her hidden in some dense bush, and it was only when one of the rangers heard her crying that they realised she was there. They found cartridges and blood and spoor from her mother, along with the hunter's tracks.'

'How awful.' I shook my head and watched her through the binoculars. Another poor animal killed unnecessarily. 'So how did she end up here?'

'I re-wilded her.'

My jaw dropped open as the binoculars fell out of my hand and landed in the footwell. 'You re-wilded her?'

'Yes. She was released here because we have a lot of lionesses and this reserve was fairly short of them.'

'But why didn't you tell me this?' I stared at him

incredulously. 'When you and Dad were having that chat about Asha when I first found her, you seemed so against the idea of me keeping her to re-wild. Why didn't you say something in all this time?'

'Because I didn't want you to think it would be easy. I know the pitfalls of trying to re-wild an animal, and I didn't want you to get this idea in your head that you could just potter about with her for a few years as a pet and everything would work out OK. It's hard. It's a long, long road, and it very rarely works to the point where an animal can survive in the wild on its own.'

'So why are you telling me now?' I asked.

He grabbed my hand and squeezed it. 'Because you've been really sad that you're not with Asha every day like before, and I wanted to show you that *this* is what you've been working towards all this time. Kira is one of the few examples of a re-wilded animal living her life, healthy and happy. She would still recognize me and my call, but for her sake, I need to just watch her and appreciate her from afar. Since she lives in a pride, there's no way I could go in there amongst them and just say hi to her. I'd probably be ripped to shreds. But I've done my job, even though I miss her like you miss Asha. When Asha has cubs of her own, she may become more distant from you as her protective instinct kicks in, but this is how things are supposed to be.'

'But I haven't been sad for Asha. I know she's intelligent and more than capable of looking after herself. I've just been sad for myself. It's like I've got this great big hole there now.'

He squeezed my hand harder. 'Believe me, I know. I still feel like that. But nothing that's worth anything in life is ever easy. If you love them, you have to let them go.'

I looked into his eyes, feeling my heart melting. Every time I'd felt sad in the last few years Zach had been there for me. He always seemed to know the right things to say. Do the right things. Make me try and become a stronger and better person. He had been a truly amazing friend, and I had been far from easy to deal with when I got to Kilingi. If it wasn't for him helping me with Asha, she probably wouldn't have been re-wilded successfully at all. I hadn't even been interested in animals. What did I know about teaching a leopard survival skills? Day after day he taught me about her needs and all about the animals out here that I hadn't given a second thought to before I arrived. I'd been too wrapped up in my own messy life to think about anyone else, but he had such strength and patience and loyalty, and he'd always gone out of his way to help me.

And that's the thing about friendship. You can really appreciate a good one when you've been let down by friends before. Good friends see you at your worst and still care about you, regardless of your faults, or ugly behaviour. Even if he'd never feel the same way about me as I did about him, I was so grateful and happy that he had ever become my friend in the first place. I would rather have him in my life as a great friend, than risk losing him if I told him how I felt. And when the time came that he did fall in love with someone, I would have to be strong enough to wish him happiness, just like I had to do with Asha.

I smiled. 'Thank you. Thank you for everything.' I didn't thank him for every individual thing he'd done. I didn't need to, and it would take all day. When he smiled and nodded, I could see by the look on his face that he understood.

'You're very welcome.' He started the Land Rover, took one more look at Kira and smiled like a proud parent. 'Now let me show you the documentary. You're going to love it!'

We got back to the lodge and I sat in the lounge with Dad, Jenna, Richard, and some of the game rangers who weren't out with the guests for the royal unveiling of the film.

I took a deep breath as I watched Asha grow on camera before my eyes from a nervous cub that fell out of the trees to a cunning and independent hunter who was an expert in stealth and agility. Her intelligence shone through in her actions as she carefully weighed up each situation and adapted to it.

It wasn't just Asha that had grown. I saw myself unfold before my eyes, too. In the beginning I was painfully shy, with that sunhat pulled low over my face and my head bowed, often turning away from the camera that I was always aware of. But as the time went on, the hat disappeared, and gradually, I held my head high, oblivious to being in the centre of attention through the lens. I had transformed into a strong, caring, and confident woman, and that's when it hit me.

Even though bad things had happened, something positive and life-changing had come out of it. I'd made peace with myself and my life, and I knew it *was* possible to heal the grief. Not just the grief of losing Mum, but the grief of losing my old self. I'd been to hell and back, and I'd emerged through the other side with a new discovery of what was important and what wasn't.

So, if you asked me now whether I believed everything happened for a reason, I'd have to say yes. Definitely, unequivocally yes.

We all cheered and hugged each other. My eyes welled up (again!), but they were tears of happiness.

'I'm so proud of you, Jazz,' Dad whispered in my ear as he gave me a tight hug. Even his eyes watered with emotion.

'That was an amazing piece of filming, Zach.' Richard clapped him on the back. 'I couldn't have done a better job myself. I've spoken to my contacts at National Geographic and they want you to send it to them as soon as you can.'

'Congratulations, Zach.' I hugged him.

Zach's face beamed with pride. 'I just hope it helps to spread the word about poaching.'

I stood up in front of them all. 'Listen, I've been thinking about that, and I've come up with a possible plan.' I began to tell them my ideas.

Chapter 27

'Have I got some amazing news for you,' Dad said with a grin when I walked into his office at the lodge to help him treat a small duiker antelope with a broken leg.

'What?'

He held a finger in the air. 'You'll have to wait. I think Zach should have the honours.'

I raised an eyebrow. 'Sounds intriguing.'

Dad got on the radio and called Zach to come to the lodge.

As Dad and I were just finishing up setting the duiker's leg in a cast, Zach strode in. He leaned casually against Dad's desk and crossed his arms, smiling at me.

'What?' I cried. 'The anticipation's killing me! What's the news?'

'The documentary aired on National Geographic Channel last week and I've had an email from someone about it.'

'Who?' I motioned for him to spit it out.

'The World Conservation Society want you to be a guest speaker at their annual fund raising event that's being held in London.'

My jaw nearly hit the floor. I pointed to my chest. 'Me? They want me?'

He nodded coolly. 'Yep.'

'Really?' I looked at Dad, who was nodding with excitement.

'There will be some really influential people there, I've been told,' Zach said. 'It's the perfect place to reveal your new plans and try and get them on board for an anti-poaching initiative. If we want to make a difference, we'll need their help.'

'Wow.' I fanned a hand in front of my face. 'I can't

believe it.'

'Are you ready to do this?' Dad asked, and I saw the worry settle on his face. 'This is a huge opportunity, but I'll completely understand if you don't want to do it.'

He was right. It was huge. And the thought of standing in front of a packed room with all eyes on me scared the crap out of me. But then the picture of Bella came into my head again, and I knew I couldn't let my fears stop me from doing the right thing. Who cared if I looked scarred or different to everyone else? This was much more important.

'I'm ready. If I can stand in front of a load of policemen waving guns at me, I can stand in front of a crowd and give a speech.' I nodded so hard I'm surprised my head didn't fall off. 'When is it?'

'In two weeks,' Dad said, 'But I won't be able to go with you. We've just heard word that another couple of rhino will be arriving then for the breeding programme, and I'll be needed here.' He nodded towards Zach. 'Zach's going to go with you. Is that OK?'

Having the greatest friend in the world with me was more than OK. 'I can't wait.' My eyes lit up. 'I'll be able to see Aunt Katrina, too!'

After we chatted excitedly about the new development, I left with Zach.

'I want to go and see Asha,' I said, which was something I did now whenever I wanted to put things into perspective. Lately, I'd allowed myself to drive closer and closer to her, and whenever she heard the Land Rover she came out to see me, her eyes lit with that same expression of love and affection she'd always had. I couldn't resist the cuddle, even if it was only for a short time. Well, I was only human.

'Want me to drive you?' Zach asked. 'I've got some time between the next game drive.'

I shook my head. 'Thanks, but I want to tell her the good news on my own.'

As I was leaving, he grabbed my hand and turned me back towards him. 'Congratulations.'

I looked up at him from behind my eyelashes. 'If it hadn't been for you, we never would have got this far.'

'Don't underestimate yourself.' He released my hand and walked off. 'Say hi to Asha for me.'

I drove to her territory, following the signal on her collar, and found her easily, dozing in a tree with the remains of a hyena carcass, looking pretty smug. And so she should be; she'd turned into an exceptional hunter.

I parked about fifty metres from the tree. 'Well, you little devil,' I said quietly to myself with a proud smile. 'Getting those annoying hyenas back, I see.'

When she saw me, her head shot up and her ears flicked back. She stretched her front legs and expertly climbed down the branches, jumping to the ground.

'Hey, Asha,' I called out.

She padded towards me, and I checked around me before getting out. I knelt down and she rubbed her head against mine. 'How've you been, my beautiful girl?'

She licked the side of my face as an answer and sat down next to me, surveying her territory, as if she were the proud daughter showing off to her mum. *Look, at this. It's all mine!*

We stayed like that for a while until I heard the unmistakable bark of a leopard. I looked up and saw a big male in the distance, watching us. Asha's ears flattened and she became instantly alert. She rose to her paws and looked between me and the male leopard, as if asking whether it was all right to go.

I pointed out to the bush. 'This is what you're here for, girl. Go.'

And with a last look over her shoulder she went to investigate. I climbed into the Land Rover and watched them approach each other, warily at first. Then Asha and the male padded closer together, and she wound her body around him. I'd seen her scent marking her territory in recent weeks, giving off a signal that she was ready to mate. Would we see the tiny patter of baby Asha paws soon, like Kira? I hoped so.

I watched for a while as they sat next to each other, nudging their heads and bodies into the other. Asha flirted with him before the male got up and wandered off into the distance with her following close behind.

I sighed softly and kept my fingers crossed for her, heading back home to start working on my speech. It had to be amazing and hard-hitting, and two weeks wasn't nearly enough time to get it ready, but there was something else I needed to do first.

I drove back to our quarters and parked outside, stopping by Asha's old enclosure and running my fingers along the bars with a smile. I went into Dad's bedroom and looked around but couldn't see it anywhere. I knew he had one around here some place.

I sat on his bed, opened the top drawer, and there it was.

Slowly, I slid my hand inside and pulled out the mirror. I heard myself suck in an involuntary breath and brought it up in front of my face.

My skin was tanned a golden colour from being out in the African sun, and the scars had faded from angry, puckered red skin to flat, pale lines. I pressed my fingers to my skin and pulled it taut, turning my head from one side to another, unable to believe how much they'd changed. Yes, I was still a girl with scars, but I wanted people to see me for what I was. The girl who'd fought for a leopard cub and won. The girl who'd stood in front of a firing squad to protect Asha. The girl who had the courage to do what was right. Everything that happened to me shaped me into what I had become, and I liked what I saw. I wasn't looking at my reflection through my own eyes anymore. I was seeing myself through the eyes of a leopard.

Chapter 28

It was strange being in England again, like being on a completely different planet. All the traffic, the noise, and everyone rushing around trying to be somewhere at a certain time was so different to life out in the bush, where time had its own definition. Spending every day immersed in the vast wilderness of Africa had become like one of the simplest, purest forms of therapy in the world, and as soon as we stepped off the plane at Heathrow I wanted to be back in Kenya. Back home with Asha, Dad, and my new family. I'd left strict instructions for Dad to call me if anything happened to her while I was away. Luckily, we were only staying in London for one night, and then we were going to see Aunt Katrina for one night before we left to go back to Kenya.

The dinner was being held at the Mayfair Plaza Hotel in London, where the owners had donated our rooms and the use of their banquet hall for the charity fundraiser. Standing in front of the mirror in my bedroom, I surveyed myself. The new simple black dress I'd bought at the shops clung to my curves like a second skin. I leaned forwards and applied eyeliner and mascara and swiped a warm peach-coloured lipstick over my lips. I was just running a hand through my long blonde hair when the phone rang.

I ran towards it, hoping it wasn't Dad calling to say something was wrong with Asha. 'Hello?' I said urgently.

'Hey, sweetheart,' Dad said.

'Please tell me Asha's OK,' I said breathlessly, flopping down onto the bed.

'Asha is just fine,' he said calmly. 'I'm calling to wish you luck.'

I breathed a sigh of relief. 'Thank God for that.' I smiled. 'Thanks Dad. I'm a bit scared. After what happened with Rebecca Swanson, I want to make sure everything I say is just right.'

'When you were reading your speech to me, I thought it was perfect,' he said.

'Thanks, that means a lot. Have the rhinos arrived yet?'

'Yes, and they're doing great after their long trip. Can't wait to release them tomorrow,' he said as someone knocked on the door.

'Sorry, Dad, but Zach's here. I have to go. Thanks so much for ringing me, and wish the rhinos luck for tomorrow.'

'Knock them dead!' he said, and we hung up.

I swung the door open to find Zach standing there in a black tuxedo, crisp white shirt, and a bow tie. His dark hair was cropped short and his jaw line smooth and oh so kissable. It was a gazillion miles away from his permanent uniform of khaki shirt, shorts, and boots, and yet he looked completely at home in it, but then Zach was one of the few people I'd ever met who was so comfortable in his own skin.

He took a step back when he saw me. 'Wow. You look stunning.'

I grinned. 'So do you.'

He came inside the room as I grabbed my black silk bag with my speech inside it.

'Are you nervous?' he asked.

'Yep.' I rubbed my stomach, trying to get rid of the butterflies beating out a heavy rock song inside. 'But I don't care.'

'That's my girl. You're going to be great. They'll love you.' He held out his hand. 'Ready?'

I slid my fingers in his. 'Absolutely. I couldn't do this without you, you know.'

His gaze met mine and he smiled. 'Come on, we don't want to be late.'

We mingled with the organisers and guests before the

dinner and then took our places at a table along with a mixture of businessmen, celebrities, politicians, and other supporters. When Zach filled my wine glass and passed it to me, our fingers touched. That familiar tingling sensation travelled up every single vertebrae, but instead of feeling regret, I felt a sensation of overwhelming happiness that he was here with me. He was on my side, and that was all I would ever need.

When the meal finished, it was time for the speakers. The first to take the podium and address the huge crowd was one of the organisers who worked for the World Wildlife Conservation Organisation. He spoke about the organisation and what projects it had been involved with so far that year. He told us about the list of species which had now become extinct, critically endangered, or endangered. I looked round the table and saw people shaking their heads with solemn expressions, or their eyes misting with compassion. There were people here who wanted to help, and together we could make a difference.

'And now we have a special guest speaker who has spent the last two years in Kenya re-wilding an orphaned leopard against great odds,' the organiser said. 'You may have seen the documentary recently shown on National Geographic Channel. Please put your hands together for Jazz Hooper.' He clapped with enthusiasm and was joined by the rest of the crowd.

I looked at Zach who winked at me.

I stood, smoothed my dress down, and walked to the podium on the stage with my head held high, clutching my speech in my right hand.

The organiser shook my hand and kissed me on the cheek. 'Jazz Hooper, ladies and gentlemen.' And he left the stage.

I unfolded my speech and flattened it against the lectern, feeling all eyes on me, and took a moment to compose myself.

You can do it, Jazz. You can do anything.

I imagined Mum standing at the back of the room, smiling

her encouragement.

I took a breath and looked up, watching the sea of eyes aimed in my direction. I smiled, and I was off...

'I'd like to thank the WWCO for inviting me here today, it's an incredible honour. Just over three years ago I was involved in a traffic accident where I sadly lost my mum. I didn't handle things very well. I was fifteen, scarred, and I thought my life was over.' I paused. 'But what happened next was a drastic and radical change that eventually put things in perspective. My dad decided to move us to Kenya, which had been my parents' home for a long time before I was born. One day I found an orphaned leopard cub that had also lost her mum, but it was poachers who tragically cut her life short, not an accident. I instantly felt a bond with this animal, whom I named Asha, and spent almost two years re-wilding her, with the help of my good friend Zach.' I smiled at him, and he beamed from ear to ear. 'If it wasn't for Asha and Zach, there's no way I'd have the confidence to stand up here and look you in the eye today.

'We recently released Asha back into the wild at Kilingi Game Reserve, and she's doing so well. She's become what she was always supposed to be: a wild animal. But the poaching of these wild animals isn't just confined to leopards. Recently on the reserve a pregnant rhino was butchered while she was still alive. Her horns were brutally hacked off and she was left to die painfully. And for what? Rhino horn is made of keratin, the same substance that's found in your hair and fingernails and has no proven scientific medical benefits.' I choked back the tears and carried on. 'Every year, thousands of animals are killed because someone, somewhere wants a piece of them. We have the fur trade, Eastern medicine, hunting for fun or sport, deforestation and loss of habitat due to an increase in human population and wars, or we keep them as pets. We're either killing them for selfish gain or loving them to death. And as you know from the list that was just read out, these animals are being pushed to extinction or endangerment.' I glanced up. Everyone's eyes were firmly fixed on me with sad expressions. 'But let me get back to poaching.' I turned the page on my notes. 'Although re-wilding with Asha worked, it's not the solution, and it's often unsuccessful. Change has to start with awareness, prevention, conservation, and protection. In some countries, even the politicians and diplomats admit to being an end user in the illegal wildlife trade, claiming that rhino horn, ivory, tiger bones, or other animal products cure everything from hangovers to cancer. This sends the price of these products sky high, and signs a death warrant for these animals. In some places, illegal animal products are worth more than gold and platinum. Until the leaders of these countries take a stand against this illegal trade, more and more of these amazing creatures will become extinct. The illegal trafficking in wild animals is now the third largest criminal industry in the world. For these animals to survive, we must make a change now. Not in two years, or one year, or even six months. The ugly truth is that some animals won't be around in six months from now. With rhinos, for example, we can't replace an animal that's been killed with enough breeding programmes because they're diminishing faster that they can reproduce. One day you'll have to show your grandchildren pictures of these animals because there will be no live ones left, unless this wildlife crisis changes drastically right now.

'The poachers now are far different from local people taking a few animals for the pot. Today, we're dealing with sophisticated organised crime syndicates who want to make money, no matter what the cost. They see these animals as a commodity to exploit. Ruthless, heavily armed people with AK47s, and in some cases, even grenades. When they're not shooting or crippling animals, they lace their food with poison and follow them until they die. Even if they track a rhino or elephant whose ivory and horn has been removed for its own safety, they will still kill the animal so they don't waste time trying to track it again. They don't care about the rangers on the reserves who protect these animals. They have one aim, and one aim only. To kill and get out as quickly as possible without getting caught. They defend themselves with enough firepower to make some armies jealous, and many rangers have died in the course of poaching activities. Many more risk their lives every day for meagre salaries.

'What we need are tougher laws in place to protect these animals, because the ones that exist are no more than just a piece of paper. We need more police and special agencies investigating this trade, and we need to enforce strict penalties. Governments need to send out strong messages that raping the land and our wild animals won't be tolerated any more. Safari tourism brings in big business, but with no animals left, these countries can kiss goodbye to it. We have to put a value on preserving wildlife, rather than killing it. We need to stop the people at the top, and we need to stop the demand for these products. We need more rangers in National Parks and on game reserves. We need more monitoring systems in place, like drones or helicopters to fly over the vast open spaces and check for suspicious activity. We need breeding programmes for endangered animals, and, because this is an international problem, we need people in the local areas to see how these animals are worth more alive, though ecotourism that provides jobs for life, than they are in an ivory trinket box, or ground up into a powder, or worn as a symbol of fashion. We need to stop corruption and complicity in wildlife trafficking at all levels.' I paused. 'But we can't just concentrate on one of these areas. We have to fight back from the bottom all the way to the top. Even if one poacher is stopped, there are hundreds more living in poverty, lured by the promise of big money, who are willing to take their place.

'All of these things cost money, but if we don't find long term solutions, our whole ecosystem will be compromised. The welfare of the human race is so closely linked to the welfare of wildlife. In saving them, we're also saving ourselves. For greed to prosper, we have to sit back and allow it.' I paused and glanced up. 'Please don't let inhumanity and indifference win the war on greed.

'Conservation has to start with people. People will only fight for what they care about, and they only care about what they know. Educating people is the first step, and at Kilingi Game Reserve, I'm going to be initiating a conservation programme to educate local tribal leaders, school children, villagers, government officials, police, and anyone interested in animal rights, because all of them are the guardians of our wildlife. Humans have had a special bond with animals for thousands of years, and in Africa, as in a lot of countries, there's a spiritual connection with them. Our aim is to work with the local communities so they won't tolerate poaching of any kind, and we need all eyes and ears to the ground to work together and inform us of any poaching activity in the area so we can try and prevent it. We will be attempting to increase awareness and understanding with them about conservation issues, promote more tolerance of animals living outside protected areas, and find practical solutions to any wildlife-human conflicts that arise. One of the big ways to make conservation work is to stimulate the local economy with tourism and provide jobs. These animals are Africa's most precious assets.

'We've also increased the number of anti-poaching teams and rangers at Kilingi. Some species on the reserve have twenty-four hour guards trailing them − a sad necessity to keep them safe. I would ask all of you to get involved. To help spread the word, help with funding to introduce programmes globally, where local people can work together with conservationists to protect these species. To help provide education and lobbying groups to tell the world exactly what is going on.

'This planet doesn't just belong to humankind, it belongs to every single creature on it, and what right do we have to decide that their lives should be cruelly stripped away?' I inhaled a breath. 'When they're gone, they're gone, and what an ugly and colourless world it would be without them in it. Right now we're living in the middle of a battle to save our planet and all the creatures that live on it.'

I looked up and saw tears rolling down some of the guests' eyes. I swallowed back the lump in my throat. 'If my words haven't touched you and prompted you to take action before it's too late, let me leave you with the words of a Cree prophecy.'

I glanced down at my notes and took a deep breath. '"When all the trees have been cut down, when all the animals have been hunted, when all the waters are polluted, when all the air is unsafe to breathe, only then will you discover you cannot eat money."' I let my gaze rest on the crowd. 'Thank you.' And as I walked away from the podium, everybody stood, clapping with so much emotion I could feel it in the air like static.

Zach held his arms out, his eyes red and watering, with a proud smile plastered firmly on his face.

I stepped into his strong arms. 'Was I OK?' I whispered.

'You were fantastic.' His lips brushed against my ear sending shock waves through every fibre of my body.

By the end of the evening, Zach and I had probably spoken to half the five hundred-strong crowd. We met many people who were trying to introduce similar education programmes in other parts of Africa and the rest of the world, and we had several offers of funding assistance for our own education programme and the protection for our animals, plus many more contact details of people who wanted to help. We stepped into the lift at two o'clock in the morning, exhausted, but ecstatic.

'What a surreal night,' I said, my mouth aching from smiling.

'You know, if I'd have told you two years ago you'd be standing up in front of all those people and talking so passionately about conservation, you'd have laughed your head off.' He shook his head slightly. 'Oh, no, wait. You didn't laugh much back then.' He pressed his thumb and forefinger to his chin, thinking. 'Actually, you probably would've punched me at the time for even suggesting it.'

I play punched him on the arm. 'There you go, just in case you think I don't care.'

'There's a bottle of champagne in the fridge in my room. I think we should celebrate.' Zach grinned at me as the lift announced its arrival on our floor with a ping.

'Sounds good to me. I'm not sure I ever want this night to end. It's been amazing.'

Zach opened the door to his room and I followed him in. He took his jacket off and slung it on the back of a chair and removed his tie, undoing the top few buttons of his shirt. 'That's better. I'm much more comfortable in my ranger's uniform.'

'I know how you feel,' I said, kicking off my high heels. 'Give me shorts and my hiking boots any day.'

He turned to the fridge and reached in for the bottle of champagne, and I stared at his back as the shirt fabric strained against his broad shoulders. When he turned back round, he caught me staring and I quickly turned my attention to the chilled glass he held out to me.

'Here.' His fingertips skimmed mine as I took it.

'Thanks.'

He popped the cork on the bottle to a loud bang and filled my glass before filling his own. 'Congratulations, Jazz. You were fantastic.' He smiled over the rim of his glass and my stomach did a flip-flop. After he'd taken a sip, he looked serious, 'I have to tell you something.'

Oh, God, what's he going to say? He's got a girlfriend?

'Sounds ominous,' I said, hoping it wouldn't be that. Anything but that. But how could I expect any different? He was a fantastic guy, and I was surprised no one had snagged his heart already.

We stared into each other's eyes for a second, and for the first time since I'd known him he looked nervous and unsure of himself. 'You're the most amazing woman I've ever met, and you don't know how much it's killed me trying not to kiss you all this time.' He looked at me with hungry, hooded eyes before setting his glass down on the table. 'You don't have any idea what a strong and sexy woman you are, do you?'

I shook my head softly in a kind of daze, unable to believe what I was hearing.

He took my glass from my hand and set it next to his before reaching out and enveloping me in his arms so my chest was pressed against the hard muscles of his torso. I could feel the heat from him seeping into every pore as he stared deep into my eyes.

Slowly, he tucked my hair behind my ear, his touch almost paralysing me. 'I'm so proud of you.'

I wanted to say thanks, but my mouth had suddenly stopped working.

He kept his eyes on mine, and I was lost in a haze of topaz as he leaned his face towards me and brushed his lips on mine.

It didn't take my mouth long to come back to life, then, I can tell you! As I opened my lips, his tongue sought mine, clashing in an urgent and passionate kiss. I could've sworn my knees were about to give away.

My brain scrambled for thoughts. I was here, kissing the most amazing man, who I'd been in love with for a long time. What was about to happen, and would it ruin our friendship?

But the next words out of his mouth told me all I needed to know.

Chapter 29

He pulled back from our first kiss with a sexy, lopsided smile on his face. Running a fingertip down my cheek with one hand, he cupped my chin with the other. 'God, I love you.'

I gasped in surprise, the shock of all that was happening turning my brain to mush. 'Y…you love me?'

He nodded firmly. 'You're the most beautiful woman I've ever known. On the inside and out. You've got such courage and determination.'

I blushed, looking into his eyes. 'I thought you said I was stubborn.'

He grinned. 'Yeah, you're that, too.'

'But…w…why didn't you tell me any of this before?' I stuttered.

'Because when you came to Kilingi you were a mess. You were grieving, angry, depressed, and your self-esteem was in the gutter. You hated yourself and everything around you. The word safari means journey, and you had to go on your own journey,' he whispered huskily. 'It wouldn't have mattered what I told you, you would've never believed me. It wouldn't have made any difference until you believed in *yourself* again. No one else can make you feel sad or happy or scared except you, and I had to let you work through it all on your own. What I saw when I looked at you was something polar opposites apart from what you felt about yourself, and until you learned to forgive and love yourself, how could you learn to love anyone else?' He stroked my face and the hairs on the back of my neck rose. 'Plus, I didn't know if you were going to stay. I didn't want anything to happen between us if you were going to go back to

England. I don't think my heart could've coped with it, and I know there aren't many women who would want to share the life I live with animals. It's too much to ask someone.'

'But you *did* make a difference to me. I've learned so much from you. You're right, it was a journey, but I couldn't have done it on my own.'

'I've learned things from you, too,' Zach said. 'You've taught me so much about bravery and determination, and how it can get you through anything in life.'

'I want that life now. With you. With the animals. Out in Africa. I can't imagine ever being anywhere else.' I slid my fingers underneath his shirt and ran them along his back, melting into him and never wanting to let him go. 'I love you, Zach. More than you can imagine.'

His lips crushed mine and my hand slid to the back of his neck.

When I pulled back for air, I whispered, 'It's my first time.'

'Are you sure this is what you want?' He gently kissed behind my ear and nuzzled his face into my neck.

I almost died of ecstasy on the spot, melting at his touch. 'Yes,' I whispered, my voice husky.

'I promise I'll be gentle.'

In between kisses we somehow moved to the bed, although I wasn't aware of it until I felt the back of the mattress against my legs because every part of my body was only aware of his touch. He pushed me gently down onto the sheets, never breaking lip contact, and I felt for the buttons on his shirt, fumbling rapidly in a rush to feel his skin against mine, in such a hurry that I only managed to release a couple of them.

He sat up and undid them slowly, staring deep into my eyes as his tanned chest came into view, and I realised that he'd never taken his shirt off in front of me before in all the time we'd been wandering around in the hot African sun.

Then I found out the reason why.

I sat up abruptly, staring at the crisscross of faint scars that ran over his chest. I touched them with my fingertips then stared up at his face, confused.

My eyes widened. 'How did you get those?'

'I made a mistake with a lion and I paid the price.' He shrugged.

'Kira?' I asked.

'Protecting Kira. When I was training her, we suddenly came across a lioness who didn't like the idea of a strange female in her territory. Before I knew what was happening, Kira and the lioness were fighting. The other lioness was bigger and stronger and had more experience, Kira was getting injured badly. Stupidly, I forgot my rifle so I couldn't fire a warning shot in the air. The only thing I could do was make as much noise as possible to try and frighten her off. So I banged the door of the Land Rover and shouted as loud as I could, but it didn't seem to scare her. Instead, she left Kira and turned her attention to me. She pounced on me, claws slicing through my skin, before Kira got a second wind and came out fighting to protect me, despite her injuries. She put up one hell of an attack which gave time for one of the rangers, who was nearby and heard what was happening, a chance to get to us and fire off some shots. I was attacked by one lion and saved by another.' He glanced down at his chest. 'This is a reminder that things don't always go to plan and you have to live every second that you have to the full.'

I rested my hand over his scars and looked up at him. 'Why didn't you tell me? You knew how I felt about mine.'

He took my hand and kissed my palm. 'It's like I told you; everybody has scars. Would it have made any difference to how you felt about me?' He looked down at me through hooded eyes.

I smiled and shook my head. 'No.'

'It doesn't define who I am, just like your scars don't define you.' He leaned over and locked me in a passionate kiss, and suddenly there was no more talking going on.

Epilogue

We followed Asha in the Land Rover and watched her climb from the bottom of the rocks to the cave we'd sheltered in from the rains all those months ago. She got to the entrance of the cave and sat there, shifting her gaze between us and something at the back.

'Why isn't she coming to see us?' I asked Zach.

He took the binoculars away from his eyes and handed them to me. 'Her protective instinct is kicking in.'

Asha walked to the rear of the cave so we could just see the end of her tail. A few moments later, she reappeared in the entrance with something in her mouth.

I pointed at the tiny bundle of fur that wriggled as Asha set it down gently on the rocks for us to see.

'She must've just had it!' I sighed happily. 'I wonder if it's a girl or a boy.'

Asha licked her newborn cub and looked at us to make sure we were watching. A proud new mother.

'What an amazing sight.' Zach draped an arm round my shoulder. 'While you were gaining a boyfriend in England, she was gaining one out here. That makes you a granny now!'

'Oi!' I squeezed Zach's hand, my heart swelling with happiness for her. 'We're so privileged to see that. No, maybe privileged is an understatement. We're blessed.'

'Maybe she's bringing the cub out to say thanks to you.'

'Seeing this is the only thanks I need.' I rested my head on his shoulder while Asha patiently cleaned and suckled her little one for hours.

I still couldn't believe she was now a mother herself. Asha. My beautiful girl, whose name meant life in Swahili. When

Zach had said all those months ago that I'd be giving her her life back, I never imagined what would happen along the way. With all my heart I hoped that she went on to live a long and happy one. But it was me who should've been thanking her, because she'd given me my life back, too.

The radio crackled, interrupting the contented scene of mother and baby. 'Jazz, come in Jazz,' Dad's voice said.

'Go ahead, Dad.'

'Can you come back to the lodge? We've had a call from the Masai Mara National Park. A female leopard was killed by poachers and they've found two of her cubs nearby. They're about four weeks old, and they're on the way here now.'

The smile dropped off my face.

I felt the fury and sadness burning deep within me like acid as I looked at Zach, who shook his head gravely.

When would the killing ever stop?

A Note from the Author

Thanks so much for buying *The See-Through Leopard*. I hope you enjoyed it. A percentage of the royalties from this book will be donated to Panthera's Anti-Poaching Campaign and various other anti-wildlife crime campaigns.

This novel came about for several reasons...

Ever since I was a kid, I was obsessed with wildlife documentaries. I even wanted to marry David Attenborough when I grew up! Every chance I got (and still do), I'd watch the spectacular footage of these animals in their natural habitats. Their beauty and intelligence never fails to amaze me. We have a unique relationship with animals. They have the ability to create so much happiness in our lives and open our hearts. I believe what we do to them, we do to humankind.

A few years ago, I read *Beautiful* by Katie Piper, an inspiring story of a courageous woman who was scarred by acid, and it got me thinking about how we live in a world where we perceive beauty based on how we look, not what we do, and how being "different" can affect someone so much. As Khalil Gibran said, "Beauty is not in the face; beauty is a light in the heart." If only we took those words on board, the world would be a much better place to live.

Then, of course, there's grief – whether it's the loss of a person, a pet, a relationship, or dream. It's something we all go through, but yet we feel so alone. There's no quick fix, and the only one that can heal yourself is you. But I wanted to show that even though it can be a long road, it is possible to heal and create fertility and positivity from grief, and sometimes our healing begins the most unexpected ways.

And then I went to Steve Irwin's Australia Zoo. I don't like zoos. I don't like seeing animals in captivity, but I'd always been so impressed with Steve Irwin and his conservation ideas. It is an educational zoo, and when I was in the tiger area, there was a lot of information about poaching and illegal wildlife trafficking, and its detrimental effects on this majestic species. And that's when all the pieces for this book clicked into place. If things carry on as they are, we won't be able to see some of these animals in the wild anymore, and I wanted to write a book that highlighted the plight that these creatures face every day. They don't have a voice, but we do.

Although this book is fiction, it's based on the sad fact that thousands of animals are dying every year due to poaching and wildlife trafficking. The only thing that stands in the way of these animals and extinction is us. Together we can all do something to stop this happening. We can help to spread the word. We can lobby our governments to provide better laws and protection. We can educate people. We can get involved with and support reputable conservation organizations. We can care enough to do something.

When they're gone, they're gone. Please don't let it be too late.

But don't take my word for it. In the following pages you can read some quotes that put these animals' lives into perspective, along with links to various conservations organizations.

Peace & Love

Sibel XX

"The fact is that no species has ever had such wholesale control over everything on earth, living or dead, as we now have. That lays upon us, whether we like it or not, an awesome responsibility. In our hands now lies not only our own future, but that of all other living creatures with whom we share the earth." – David Attenborough

"The global value of illegal wildlife trade is between $7.8 billion and $10 billion per year. It is a major illicit transnational activity worldwide—along with arms, drugs and human trafficking. High-level traders and kingpins are rarely arrested, prosecuted, convicted or punished for their crimes.

Even more worrying, these species cannot survive high levels of poaching for long."
SOURCE – WWF

"Leopards are one of the most persecuted big cats as a result of retaliatory killing by livestock owners, poorly managed trophy hunting, and illegal hunting for fur and body parts for the commercial trade in Asia. Leopards are now extinct in 6 countries which they formerly occupied, and their presence in 6 additional countries is very uncertain." SOURCE – PANTHERA

"In the 1960s an estimated 70,000 black rhinos were found in Africa and in 1981 the numbers had dropped to around 15,000, and only twelve years later, slightly more than 2000 of the population remained. The main cause of decline is poaching and the demand for its horn." SOURCE -- EARTH'S ENDANGERED CREATURES

"Lions have vanished from over 80% of their historic range." SOURCE – PANTHERA

"Over the past 50 years Africa's lion populations have plummeted from over 200,000 individuals back in the 1960's to fewer than 25,000 today.

While many factors are listed as contributory to the overall decline in lion population numbers (including loss of habitat, conflict with growing human and livestock populations, declines in the number of functioning protected areas, etc), trophy hunting is a highly significant and immediately preventable source of additive mortality. The CITES Trade Database lists a total of 6,652 lion trophies exported 2000-2009, virtually all males." SOURCE − LION AID

"Today, tigers persist in only 7% of their historical range. One hundred years ago, as many as 100,000 wild tigers roamed the forests and grasslands of Asia. Today, fewer than 3,200 tigers remain in the wild in 13 countries."
SOURCE − PANTHERA

"In the last century elephant populations massively declined due to habitat destruction, increased agriculture and the bloody ivory trade. Rampant ivory poaching from 1979 to 1989 halved Africa's elephant population from 1.3 million to 600,000. Today numbers may be as low as 470,000."
SOURCE − BORN FREE FOUNDATION

"Some 24,000 of the continent's remaining lions are primarily in 10 strongholds: 4 in East Africa and 6 in southern Africa, the researchers determined. Over 6,000 of the remaining lions are in populations of doubtful long-term viability. Lion populations in West and central Africa are the most acutely threatened, with many recent local extinctions, even in nominally protected areas." SOURCE −
NATIONAL GEOGRAPHIC

"Revered as the planet's fastest land animal, there are estimated to be fewer than 10,000 adult individuals left in the wild. Cheetahs once inhabited the whole African continent except for the Congo Basin rainforest. Today, they have vanished from over 77 percent of their historic range in Africa." SOURCE – PANTHERA

"The five remaining subspecies of tiger are all 'endangered', African lions are officially 'vulnerable' and the Asiatic lion is 'endangered'. Africa's leopard subspecies are not considered in immediate danger of extinction but Asia's leopard subspecies are all 'endangered'. The Jaguar is 'near threatened'." SOURCE – BORN FREE FOUNDATION

"It is estimated that approximately 3,500 wild tigers remain in the world, and numbers of this iconic species are continuing to decrease." SOURCE – BORN FREE FOUNDATION

Conservation Links:

http://www.panthera.org/

http://www.rewildingfoundation.org/

http://www.bornfree.org.uk/

http://www.georgeadamson.org/

http://www.snowleopard.org/

http://www.tusk.org/

http://www.savetherhino.org/

http://animals.nationalgeographic.com/animals/big-cats/cause-an-uproar/

http://www.ifaw.org/european-union

http://www.wwf.org/

http://worldlionday.com/associates/

http://www.cheetah.org/

The See-Through Leopard
Sibel Hodge

Copyright © Sibel Hodge 2013

CPSIA information can be obtained at www.ICGtesting.com
Printed in the USA
LVOW07s1549280615

444184LV00004B/239/P